Selenium WebDriver Re

The problem solving guide to Selenium WebDriver in Ruby

Zhimin Zhan

Selenium WebDriver Recipes in Ruby

The problem solving guide to Selenium WebDriver in Ruby

Zhimin Zhan

This book is for sale at
http://www.amazon.com/Selenium-WebDriver-Recipes-Ruby-problem/dp/1505885329

This version was published on 2016-02-02

ISBN 978-1-50-588532-3

Leanpub

This is a Leanpub book. Leanpub empowers authors and publishers with the Lean Publishing process. Lean Publishing is the act of publishing an in-progress ebook using lightweight tools and many iterations to get reader feedback, pivot until you have the right book and build traction once you do.

Also By Zhimin Zhan

Practical Web Test Automation

Watir Recipes

Selenium WebDriver Recipes in Java

Learn Ruby Programming by Examples

Selenium WebDriver Recipes in Python

To Dominic and Courtney!

Contents

Preface i
    Who should read this book ii
    How to read this book ii
    Recipe test scripts ii
    Send me feedback ii

1. **Introduction** 1
    Selenium 1
    Selenium language bindings: Java, C#, Python and Ruby 1
    Cross browser testing 4
    RSpec 7
    Run recipe scripts 11

2. **Locating web elements** 17
    Start browser 17
    Find element by ID 18
    Find element by Name 18
    Find element by Link Text 18
    Find element by Partial Link Text 18
    Find element by XPath 19
    Find element by Tag Name 20
    Find element by Class 21
    Find element by CSS Selector 21
    Chain find_element to find child elements 21
    Find multiple elements 22

3. **Hyperlink** 23
    Click a link by text 23
    Click a link by ID 23

Click a link by partial text 23
Click a link by XPath 24
Click Nth link with exact same label 25
Verify a link present or not? 25
Getting link data attributes 26
Test links open a new browser window 26

4. **Button** **29**
Click a button by text 29
Click a form button by text 29
Submit a form 30
Click a button by ID 30
Click a button by name 31
Click a image button 31
Click a button via JavaScript 31
Assert a button present 31
Assert a button enabled or disabled? 32

5. **TextField and TextArea** **33**
Enter text into a text field by name 33
Enter text into a text field by ID 33
Enter text into a password field 33
Clear a text field 34
Enter text into a multi-line text area 34
Assert value 34
Focus on a control 34
Set a value to a read-only or disabled text field 35
Set and assert the value of a hidden field 35

6. **Radio button** **37**
Select a radio button 37
Clear radio option selection 37
Assert a radio option is selected 38
Iterate radio buttons in a radio group 38
Click Nth radio button in a group 39
Click radio button by the following label 39
Customized Radio buttons - iCheck 40

7. **CheckBox** **43**

Select by name 43
Uncheck a checkbox 43
Assert a checkbox is checked (or not) 44
Customized Checkboxes - iCheck 44

8. **Select List** 47
Select an option by text 47
Select an option by value 47
Select an option by iterating all options 48
Select multiple options 48
Clear one selection 48
Clear selection 49
Assert selected option 49
Assert the value of a select list 49
Assert multiple selections 50

9. **Navigation and Browser** 51
Go to a URL 51
Visit pages within a site 51
Perform actions from right mouse click context menu such as 'Back', 'Forward'
    or 'Refresh' 52
Open browser in certain size 52
Maximize browser window 52
Move browser window 52
Minimize browser window 53
Scroll focus to control 53
Switch between browser windows or tabs 53
Remember current web page URL, then come back to it later 54

10. **Assertion** 55
Assert page title 55
Assert Page Text 55
Assert Page Source 56
Assert Label Text 56
Assert Span text 56
Assert Div text or HTML 57
Assert Table text 58
Assert text in a table cell 59
Assert text in a table row 59

Assert image present 59

11. Frames 61
Testing Frames 61
Testing IFrame 62
Test multiple iframes 63

12. Testing AJAX 65
Wait within a time frame 65
Explicit Waits until Time out 66
Implicit Waits until Time out 66
Create your own polling check function 66
Wait AJAX Call to complete using JQuery 68

13. File Upload and Popup dialogs 71
File upload 71
JavaScript pop ups 72
Modal style dialogs 73
Bypass basic authentication by embedding username and password in URL . . . 74
Timeout on an operation 74
Internet Explorer modal dialog 75
Popup Handler Approach 75
Handle JavaScript dialog with Popup Handler 76
Basic or Proxy Authentication Dialog 77

14. Debugging Test Scripts 79
Print text for debugging 79
Write text to IDE output 79
Write page source or element HTML into a file 80
Take screenshot 80
Using IRB 81
Leave browser open after test finishes 82
Pause/Stop test execution at certain step 82
Run selected test steps against current browser 83

15. Test Data 85
Get date dynamically 85
Get a random boolean value 86
Generate a number within a range 86

Get a random character 87
Get a random string at fixed length 87
Get a random string in a collection 87
Generate random person names, emails, addresses with Faker 88
Generate a test file at fixed sizes 88
Retrieve data from Database 89

16. **Browser Profile and Capabilities** **91**
Get browser type and version 91
Set HTTP Proxy for Browser 91
Verify file download in Chrome 92
Test downloading PDF in Firefox 93
Bypass basic authentication with Firefox AutoAuth plugin 93
Manage Cookies 95
Headless browser testing with PhantomJS 95
Test responsive websites 96

17. **Advanced User Interactions** **97**
Double click a control 97
Move mouse to a control - Mouse Over 98
Click and hold - select multiple items 98
Context Click - right click a control 98
Drag and drop 99
Drag slider 100
Send key sequences - Select All and Delete 100

18. **HTML 5 and JavaScript** **103**
HTML5 Email type field 103
HTML5 Time Field 103
Invoke 'onclick' JavaScript event 104
Invoke JavaScript events such as 'onchange' 105
Scroll to the bottom of a page 105
Chosen - Standard Select 106
Chosen - Multiple Select 108
AngularJS web pages 112
Ember JS web pages 113
"Share Location" with Firefox 114
Faking Geolocation with JavaScript 116

19. **WYSIWYG HTML editors** **117**
    TinyMCE 117
    CKEditor 118
    SummerNote 119
    CodeMirror 120

20. **Leverage Programming** **123**
    Raise exceptions to fail test 123
    Ignorable test statement error 125
    Read external file 125
    Data-Driven Tests with Excel 126
    Data-Driven Tests with CSV 127
    Identify element IDs with dynamically generated long prefixes 128
    Sending special keys such as Enter to an element or browser 128
    Use of unicode in test scripts 129
    Extract a group of dynamic data : verify search results in order 130
    Verify uniqueness of a set of data 131
    Extract dynamic visible data rows from a results table 131
    Extract dynamic text following a pattern using Regex 133
    Quick extract pattern text in comments with Regex 134

21. **Optimization** **137**
    Assert text in page_source is faster than the text 137
    Getting text from more specific element is faster 138
    Avoid programming if-else block code if possible 138
    Use variable to cache not-changed data 139
    Enter large text into a text box 140
    Use Environment Variables to change test behaviours dynamically 140
    Test web site in two languages 141
    Multi-language testing with lookups 143

22. **Gotchas** **145**
    Test starts browser but no execution with blank screen 145
    Failed to assert copied text in browser 146
    The same test works for Chrome, but not for IE 147
    "unexpected tag name 'input'" 148
    Element is not clickable or not visible 149
    Lack knowledge of the programming language 149

23. **Extend Selenium** **151**
    Watir-WebDriver 151
    RWebSpec 152

24. **Selenium with Cucumber** **157**
    How Selenium-WebDriver is integrated with Cucumber? 157
    Execute Cucumber tests 159
    Cucumber or RSpec? 161

25. **Selenium Remote Control Server** **163**
    Selenium Server Installation 163
    Execute tests in specified browser on another machine 164
    Selenium Grid 165

Afterword **169**

Resources **173**
    Books 173
    Web Sites 174
    Tools 174

Preface

After observing many failed test automation attempts by using expensive commercial test automation tools, I am delighted to see that the value of open-source testing frameworks has finally been recognized. I still remember the day (a rainy day at a Gold Coast hotel in 2011) when I found out that the Selenium WebDriver was the most wanted testing skill in terms of the number of job ads on the Australia's top job-seeking site.

Now Selenium WebDriver is big in the testing world. Software giants such as Facebook and LinkedIn use it, immensely-comprehensive automated UI testing enables them pushing out releases several times a day[1]. However, from my observation, many software projects, while using Selenium, are not getting much value from test automation, and certainly nowhere near its potential. A clear sign of this is that the regression testing is not conducted on a daily basis (if test automation is done well, it will happen naturally).

Among the factors contributing to test automation failures, a key one is that automation testers lack sufficient knowledge in the test framework. It is quite common to see some testers or developers get excited when they first create a few simple test cases and see them run in a browser. However, it doesn't take long for them to encounter some obstacles: such as being unable to automate certain operations. If one step cannot be automated, the whole test case does not work, which is the nature of test automation. Searching solutions online is not always successful, and posting questions on forums and waiting can be frustrating (usually, very few people seek professional help from test automation coaches). Not surprisingly, many projects eventually gave up test automation or just used it for testing a handful of scenarios.

The motivation of this book is to help motivated testers work better with Selenium. The book contains over 160 recipes for web application tests with Selenium. If you have read one of my other books: 'Practical Web Test Automation[2]', you probably know my style: practical. I will let the test scripts do most of the talking. These recipe test scripts are 'live', as I have created the target test site and included offline test web pages. With both, you can:

1. **Identify** your issue
2. **Find** the recipe
3. **Run** the test case
4. **See** test execution in your browser

---

[1]http://www.wired.com/business/2013/04/linkedin-software-revolution/
[2]https://leanpub.com/practical-web-test-automation

Who should read this book

This book is for testers or programmers who write (or want to learn) automated tests with Selenium WebDriver. In order to get the most of this book, basic Ruby coding skill is required.

How to read this book

Usually, a 'recipe' book is a reference book. Readers can go directly to the part that interests them. For example, if you are testing a multiple select list and don't know how, you can look up in the Table of Contents, then go to the chapter. This book supports this style of reading.

If you are new to Selenium WebDriver, I recommend you to try out the recipes from the front to back. The best way to learn test automation is by doing it. The test web pages, test sites and the recipe test scripts are available on the book site[3]. The recipes in the first half of the book are arranged according to their levels of complexity, I believe readers can get the pattern of testing with Selenium and gain confidence after going through them.

Recipe test scripts

To help readers to learn more effectively, this book has a dedicated site[4] which contains the sample test scripts and related resources.

As an old saying goes, "There's more than one way to skin a cat." You can achieve the same testing outcome with test scripts implemented in different ways. The recipe test scripts in this book are written for simplicity, and there is always room for improvement. But for many, to understand the solution quickly and get the job done are probably more important.

If you have a better and simpler way, please let me know.

All recipe test scripts are Selenium 2 (aka Selenium WebDriver) compliant, and can be run on Firefox, Chrome and Internet Explorer on multiple platforms. I plan to keep the test scripts updated with the latest stable Selenium version.

Send me feedback

I would appreciate your comments, suggestions, reports on errors in the book and the recipe test scripts. You may submit your feedback on the book's site.

---

[3]http://zhimin.com/books/selenium-recipes
[4]http://zhimin.com/books/selenium-recipes

Zhimin Zhan

March 2014

1. Introduction

Selenium is a free and open source library for automated testing web applications. I assume that you have had some knowledge of Selenium, based on the fact that you picked up this book (or opened it in your eBook reader).

Selenium

Selenium was originally created in 2004 by Jason Huggins, who was later joined by his other ThoughtWorks colleagues. Selenium supports all major browsers and tests can be written in many programming languages and run on Windows, Linux and Macintosh platforms.

Selenium 2 is merged with another test framework WebDriver (that's why you see 'selenium-webdriver') led by Simon Stewart at Google (update: Simon now works at FaceBook), Selenium 2.0 was released in July 2011.

Selenium language bindings: Java, C#, Python and Ruby

Selenium tests can be written in multiple programming languages such as Java, C#, Python and Ruby (the core ones). Quite commonly, I heard the saying such as *"This is a Java project, so we shall write tests in Java as well"*. I disagree. Software testing is to verify whether programmer's work meets customer's needs. In a sense, testers are representing customers. Testers should have more weight on deciding the test syntax than programmers. Plus, why would you mandate that your testers should have the same programming language skills as the programmers. In my subjective view, scripting languages such as Ruby and Python are more suitable for test scripts than compiled languages such as C# and Java (Confession: I have been programming in Java for over 10 years). By the way, we call them test scripts, for a reason.

All examples in this book are written in Selenium with Ruby binding. This does not mean this book is limited to testers/developers who know Ruby. As you will see the examples below, the use of Selenium in different bindings are very similar. Once you master one, you can apply it to others quite easily. Take a look at a simple Selenium test script in four different language bindings: Java, C#, Python and Ruby.

Java:

```java
import org.openqa.selenium.By;
import org.openqa.selenium.WebDriver;
import org.openqa.selenium.WebElement;
import org.openqa.selenium.firefox.FirefoxDriver;

public class GoogleSearch {
  public static void main(String[] args) {
    // Create a new instance of the html unit driver
    // Notice that the remainder of the code relies on the interface,
    // not the implementation.
    WebDriver driver = new FirefoxDriver();

    // And now use this to visit Google
    driver.get("http://www.google.com");

    // Find the text input element by its name
    WebElement element = driver.findElement(By.name("q"));

    // Enter something to search for
    element.sendKeys("Hello Selenium WebDriver!");

    // Submit the form based on an element in the form
    element.submit();

    // Check the title of the page
    System.out.println("Page title is: " + driver.getTitle());
  }
}
```

C#:

```
using System;
using OpenQA.Selenium;
using OpenQA.Selenium.Firefox;
using OpenQA.Selenium.Support.UI;

class GoogleSearch
{
  static void Main()
  {
    IWebDriver driver = new FirefoxDriver();
    driver.Navigate().GoToUrl("http://www.google.com");
    IWebElement query = driver.FindElement(By.Name("q"));
    query.SendKeys("Hello Selenium WebDriver!");
    query.Submit();
    Console.WriteLine(driver.Title);
  }
}
```

Python:

```python
from selenium import webdriver

driver = webdriver.Firefox()
driver.get("http://www.google.com")

elem = driver.find_element_by_name("q")
elem.send_keys("Hello WebDriver!")
elem.submit()

print(driver.title)
```

Ruby:

```
require "selenium-webdriver"

driver = Selenium::WebDriver.for :firefox
driver.navigate.to "http://www.google.com"

element = driver.find_element(:name, 'q')
element.send_keys "Hello Selenium WebDriver!"
element.submit

puts driver.title
```

Cross browser testing

The biggest advantage of Selenium over other web test frameworks, in my opinion, is that it supports all major web browsers: Firefox, Chrome and Internet Explorer. The browser market nowadays is more diversified (based on the StatsCounter[1], the usage share in November 2014 for Chrome, IE and Firefox are 51.8%, 21.7% and 18.5% respectively). It is logical that all external facing web sites require serious cross-browser testing. Selenium is a natural choice for this purpose, as it far exceeds other commercial tools and free test frameworks.

Firefox

Selenium supports Firefox out of the box, i.e., as long as you have Firefox (and a not too outdated version) installed, you are ready to go. The test script below (in a file named: *ch01_-open_firefox.rb*) will open a web site in a new Firefox window.

```
require 'selenium-webdriver'
driver = Selenium::WebDriver.for(:firefox)
driver.navigate.to("http://testwisely.com/demo")
```

For readers who can't wait to see the test running, below is the command you need to use to execute a test, which you can download from the book's site (Ruby and *selenium-webdriver* gem need to be installed first. See instructions towards the end of this chapter).

---

[1]http://en.wikipedia.org/wiki/Usage_share_of_web_browsers

```
> ruby ch01_open_firefox.rb
```

Chrome

To run Selenium tests in Google Chrome, besides the Chrome browser itself, *ChromeDriver* needs to be installed.

Installing ChromeDriver is easy: go to ChromeDriver site[2].

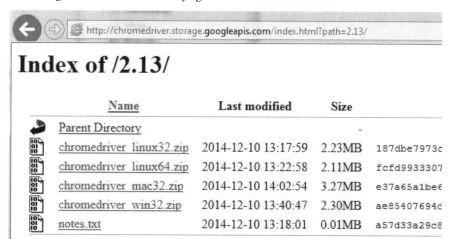

Download the one for your target platform, unzip it and put **chromedriver** executable in your PATH. To verify the installation, open a command window (terminal for Unix/Mac), execute command *chromedriver*, You shall see:

```
C:\>chromedriver
Starting ChromeDriver 2.13.307647 (5a7d0541ebc58e69994a6fb2ed930f45261f3c29) on port 9515
Only local connections are allowed.
```

The test script below opens a site in a new Chrome browser window and closes it one second later.

```ruby
require 'selenium-webdriver'
driver = Selenium::WebDriver.for(:chrome)
driver.navigate.to("http://testwisely.com/demo")
sleep 1 # wait 1 second
driver.quit
```

---

[2]https://sites.google.com/a/chromium.org/chromedriver/downloads

Internet Explorer

Selenium requires IEDriverServer to drive IE browser. Its installation process is very similar to *chromedriver*. IEDriverServer is available at http://www.seleniumhq.org/download/[3]. Choose the right one based on your windows version (32 or 64 bit).

> Download version 2.44.0 for (recommended) 32 bit Windows IE or 64 bit Windows IE
> CHANGELOG

When a tests starts to execute in IE, before navigating the target test site, you will see this first:

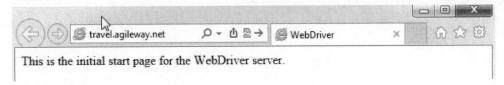

If you get this on IE9: "Unexpected error launching Internet Explorer. Protected Mode must be set to the same value (enabled or disabled) for all zones." Go to 'Internet Options', select each zone (as illustrated below) and make sure they are all set to the same mode (protected or not).

---

[3]http://www.seleniumhq.org/download/

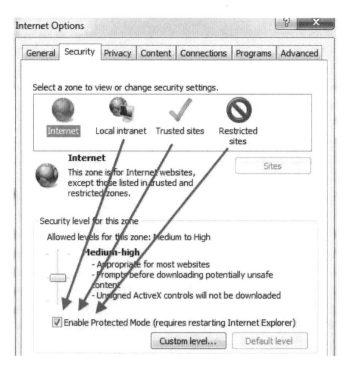

Further configuration is required for IE10 and IE11, see IE and IEDriverServer Runtime Configuration[4] for details.

```
require 'selenium-webdriver'
driver = Selenium::WebDriver.for(:ie)
driver.navigate.to("http://testwisely.com/demo")
```

RSpec

Selenium drives browsers. However, to make the effective use of Selenium scripts for testing, we need to put them in a test framework that defines test structures and provides assertions (performing checks in test scripts). Typical choices are:

- xUnit Unit Test Frameworks such as JUnit (for Java), NUnit (for C#) and minitest (for Ruby).
- Behaviour Driven Frameworks such as RSpec and Cucumber (for Ruby).

---

[4]https://code.google.com/p/selenium/wiki/InternetExplorerDriver#Required_Configuration

In this book, I use RSpec, the de facto Behaviour Driven Development (BDD) framework for
Ruby. Here is an example.

```ruby
require 'selenium-webdriver'

describe "Selenium Recipes - Start different browsers" do

  it "Start Chrome" do
    driver = Selenium::WebDriver.for(:chrome)
    driver.navigate.to("http://travel.agileway.net")
    sleep 1
    driver.quit
  end

  it "Start FireFox" do
    driver = Selenium::WebDriver.for(:firefox)
    driver.navigate.to("http://travel.agileway.net")
    expect(driver.title).to eq("Agile Travel")
    sleep 1
    driver.quit
  end

  it "Start IE" do
    driver = Selenium::WebDriver.for(:ie)
    driver.get("http://travel.agileway.net")
    sleep 1
    expect(driver.page_source).to include("User Name")
    driver.quit
  end

end
```

The keywords `describe` and `it` define the structure of a test script.

- **describe "..."** do

    Description of a collection of related test cases

- `it "..." do`

    Individual test case.

`expect().to` statements are called rspec-expectations, which are used to perform checks (also known as assertions).

> ## RSpec's old "should-based" expectation syntax
>
> There is also an older `should-based` syntax, which is still supported in RSpec 3 but deprecated. Here is the `should-syntax` version of the above example:
>
> ```
> driver.title.should == "Selenium Recipes"
> driver.title.include?("Selenium").should be_truthy
> driver.title.include?("Selenium").should_not be_falsey
> driver.title.should_not include("Watir")
> ```

Typical RSpec test script

The above example test script shows the basic structure and assertions in RSpec. However, we typically don't write a test case explicitly for multiple browsers, instead, we focus on test scenarios like below.

```
load File.dirname(__FILE__) + '/../test_helper.rb'

describe "Selenium Recipes - Start different browsers" do
  include TestHelper

  before(:all) do
    @driver = Selenium::WebDriver.for(:chrome)
  end

  before(:each) do
    @driver.navigate.to("http://travel.agileway.net")
  end
```

```
after(:all) do
  @driver.quit
end

it "Invalid Login" do
  @driver.find_element(:id, "username").send_keys("agileway")
  @driver.find_element(:id, "password").send_keys("changeme")
  @driver.find_element(:xpath,"//input[@value='Sign in']").click
  expect(@driver.page_source).to include("Invalid email or password")
end

it "Login successfully" do
  @driver.find_element(:id, "username").send_keys("agileway")
  @driver.find_element(:id, "password").send_keys("testwise")
  @driver.find_element(:xpath,"//input[@value='Sign in']").click
  expect(@driver.page_source).to include("Signed in!")
end

end
```

In this test script, we see another RSpec feature.

- **before()** and **after()** hooks.

  Optional test statements run before and after each or all test cases. Use these hooks effectively can help you writing the test scripts that are more concise and easier to maintain.

You will find more about RSpec from its home page[5]. However, I honestly don't think it is necessary. The part used for test scripts is not much and quite intuitive. After studying and trying out some examples, you will be quite comfortable with RSpec.

As a general good practice, all test scripts include a common test helper (include TestHelper) which loads required libraries and defines a set of reusable functions that are available to all test cases. For more on designing maintainable test scripts, refer to my other book: *Practical Web Test Automation*[6].

---

[5]http://rspec.info
[6]https://leanpub.com/practical-web-test-automation

Run recipe scripts

Test scripts for all recipes can be downloaded from the book site. They are all in ready-to-run state. I include the target web pages/sites as well as Selenium test scripts. There are two kinds of target web pages: local HTML files and web pages on a live site. Running tests written for a live site requires Internet connection.

Run tests in TestWise

TestWise is a functional testing Integration Development Environment (IDE) that supports Selenium and Watir (another popular web test library, used for testing Internet Explorer). TestWise community edition is free of charge.

In this book, I refer to TestWise when editing or executing test scripts. If you have a preferred testing tools or IDE, such as Apatana Studio and NetBeans 6, go for it. It shall not affect your learning this book or running recipe test scripts.

Installing TestWise is easy. It only takes a couple of minutes (unless your Internet speed is very slow) to download and install. And TestWise is the only software you need to use while learning with this book (or developing Selenium test scripts for your work). Using it is likely to make it easier for you to focus on learning Selenium.

To open recipe test scripts (after you download the recipe tests (a zip file) from the book site and unzip to a folder), close the currently opened project if there is one. Select menu File → Open Project,

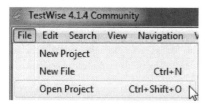

select the project file *selenium-recipes-scripts\selenium-recipes-samples.tpr*

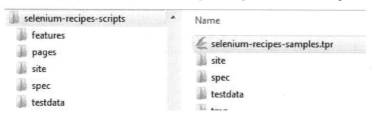

The TestWise window (after loading a test project) should look like the following:

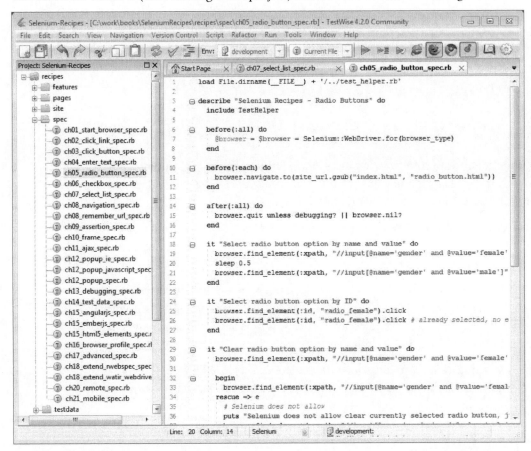

Find a test case

You can locate the recipe either by following the chapter or searching by name. There are over 100 test cases in one test project. Here is the quickest way to find the one you want in TestWise.

Select menu 'Navigation' → 'Go to Test Case..'.

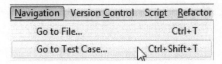

A pop up window lists all test cases in the project for your selection. The finding starts as soon as you type.

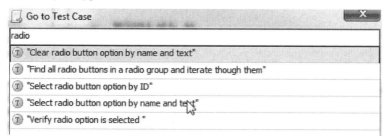

Within a test script file (opened in the editor), press Ctrl+F12 to show and select test cases inside it.

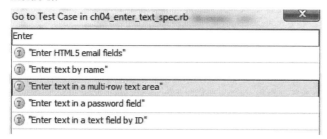

Run individual test case

Move caret to a line within a test case (between it "..." do and end). Right mouse click and select "Run '...'".

```
it "Verify checkbox is selected" do
  the_checkbox = browser.find_element(:name => "vehicle_bike")
  the_checkbox.click unless the_checkbox.selected?
  expect(the_checkbox.selected?).to be_truthy
  the_checkbox.click
  expect(the_checkbox.selected?).to be_falsey
end
```

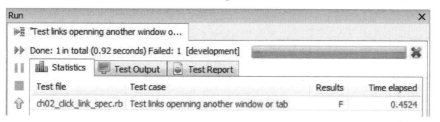

The below is a screenshot of execution panel when one test case failed,

Test file	Test case	Results	Time elapsed
ch02_click_link_spec.rb	Test links openning another window or tab	F	0.4524

Run all test cases in a test script file

You can also run all test cases in the currently opened test script file by clicking the blue triangle button on the tool bar.

The below is a screenshot of the execution panel when all test cases in a test script file passed,

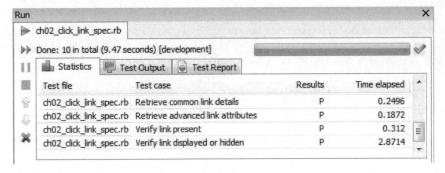

Run tests from command line

One advantage of open-source test frameworks, such as Selenium, is FREEDOM. You can edit the test scripts in any text editors and run them from a command line.

You need to install Ruby first, then install RSpec and your preferred web test driver and library (known as Gem in Ruby). Basic steps are:

- install Ruby interpreter

  Window installer: http://rubyinstaller.org, Linux/Mac: included or compile from source
- install RSpec

  > *gem install rspec*
- install test framework gem(s)

  > *gem install selenium-webdriver*

For windows users, you may simply download and install the free pre-packaged RubyShell (based on Ruby Windows Installer) at testwisely.com[7].

---

[7]http://testwisely.com/testwise/downloads

Once the installation (takes about 1 minute) is complete, we can run an RSpec test from the command line. You need to have some knowledge of typing commands in a console (Unix) or command window.

To run test cases in a test script file (named *google_spec.rb*), enter command

```
> rspec google_spec.rb
```

Run multiple test script files in one go:

```
> rspec first_spec.rb  second_test.rb
```

Run an individual test case in a test script file, supply a line number in a chosen test case range.

```
> rspec google_spec.rb:30
```

To generate a test report (HTML) after test execution:

```
> rspec -fh google_spec.rb > test_report.html
```

The command syntax is identical for Mac OS X and Linux platforms.

2. Locating web elements

As you might have already figured out, to drive an element in a page, we need to find it first. Selenium uses what is called locators to find and match the elements on web page. There are 8 locators in Selenium:

Locator	Example
ID	`find_element(:id, "user")`
Name	`find_element(:name, "username")`
Link Text	`find_element(:link_text, "Login")`
	`find_element(:link, "Login")`
Partial Link Text	`find_element(:partial_link_text, "Next")`
XPath	`find_element(:xpath, "//div[@id="login"]/input")`
Tag Name	`find_element(:tag_name, "body")`
Class Name	`find_element(:class_name, "table")`
	`find_element(:class, "body")`
CSS	`find_element(:css, "#login > input[type="text"]")`

You may use any one of them to narrow down the element you are looking for.

Start browser

Testing websites starts with a browser.

```
require 'selenium-webdriver'
driver = Selenium::WebDriver.for(:firefox)
driver.navigate.to("http://testwisely.com/demo")
```

Use `:chrome` and `:ie` for testing in Chrome and IE respectively.

I recommend, for beginners, to close the browser window at the end of a test case.

```
driver.quit # or driver.close
```

Find element by ID

Using IDs is the easiest and the safest way to locate an element in HTML. If the page is W3C HTML conformed[1], the IDs should be unique and identified in web controls. In comparison to texts, test scripts that use IDs are less prone to application changes (e.g. developers may decide to change the label, but are less likely to change the ID).

```
driver.find_element(:id, "submit_btn").click    # Button
driver.find_element(:id, "cancel_link").click   # Link
driver.find_element(:id, "username").send_keys("agileway")  # Textfield
driver.find_element(:id, "alert_div").text      # HTML Div element
```

Find element by Name

The name attributes are used in form controls such as text fields and radio buttons. The values of the name attributes are passed to the server when a form is submitted. In terms of least likelihood of a change, the name attribute is probably only second to ID.

```
driver.find_element(:name, "comment").send_keys("Selenium Cool")
```

Find element by Link Text

For Hyperlinks only. Using a link's text is probably the most direct way to click a link, as it is what we see on the page.

```
driver.find_element(:link_text, "Cancel").click
```

Find element by Partial Link Text

Selenium allows you to identify a hyperlink control with a partial text. This can be quite useful when the text is dynamically generated. In other words, the text on one web page might be different on your next visit. We might be able to use the common text shared by these dynamically generated link texts to identify them.

---

[1]http://www.w3.org/TR/WCAG20-TECHS/H93.html

```
# will click the "Cancel" link
driver.find_element(:partial_link_text, "ance").click
```

Find element by XPath

XPath, the XML Path Language, is a query language for selecting nodes from an XML document. When a browser renders a web page, it parses it into a DOM tree or similar. XPath can be used to refer a certain node in the DOM tree. If this sounds a little too much technical for you, don't worry, just remember XPath is the most powerful way to find a specific web control.

```
# clicking the checkbox under 'div2' container
driver.find_element(:xpath, "//*[@id='div2']/input[@type='checkbox']").click
```

Some testers feel intimidated by the complexity of XPath. However, in practice, there is only limited scope of XPath to master for testers.

Avoid using copied XPath from Browser's Developer Tool

Browser's Developer Tool (right click to select 'Inspect element' to show) is very useful for identifying a web element in web page. You may get the XPath of a web element there, as shown below (in Chrome):

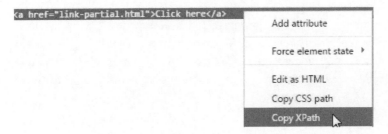

The copied XPath for the second "Click here" link in the example is:

```
//*[@id="container"]/div[3]/div[2]/a
```

It works. However, I do not recommend this approach as the test script is fragile. If developer adds another div under `<div id='container'>`, the copied XPath is no longer correct for the element while `//div[contains(text(), "Second")]/a[text()="Click here"]` still works.

In summary, XPath is a very powerful way to locate web elements when `:id`, `:name` or `:link_text` are not applicable. Try to use a XPath expression that is less vulnerable to structure changes around the web element.

Find element by Tag Name

There are a limited set of tag names in HTML. In other words, many elements share the same tag names on a web page. We normally don't use the `tag_name` locator by itself to locate an element. We often use it with others in a chained locators (see the section below). However, there is an exception.

```
driver.find_element(:tag, "body").text
```

The above test statement returns the text view of a web page. This is a very useful one as Selenium WebDriver does not have built-in method to return the text of a web page.

Find element by Class

The class attribute of a HTML element is used for styling. It can also be used for identifying elements. Commonly, a HTML element's class attribute has multiple values, like below.

```
<a href="back.html" class="btn btn-default">Cancel</a>
<input type="submit" class="btn btn-deault btn-primary">Submit</input>
```

You may use any one of them.

```
driver.find_element(:class, "btn-primary").click  # Submit button
driver.find_element(:class, "btn").click          # Cancel link


# the below will return error "Compound class names not permitted"
# driver.find_element(:class, "btn btn-deault btn-primary").click
```

The class locator is convenient for testing JavaScript/CSS libraries (such as TinyMCE) which typically use a set of defined class names.

```
# inline editing
driver.find_element(:id, "client_notes").click
sleep
driver.find_element(:class, "editable-textarea").send_keys("inline notes")
sleep 0.5
driver.find_element(:class, "editable-submit").click
```

Find element by CSS Selector

You may also use CSS Path to locate a web element.

```
driver.find_element(:css, "#div2 > input[type='checkbox']").click
```

However, the use of CSS selector is generally more prone to structure changes of a web page.

Chain find_element to find child elements

For a page containing more than one elements with the same attributes, like the one below, we could use XPath locator.

```
<div id="div1">
  <input type="checkbox" name="same" value="on"> Same checkbox in Div 1
</div>
<div id="div2">
  <input type="checkbox" name="same" value="on"> Same checkbox in Div 2
</div>
```

There is another way: chain `find_element` to find a child element.

```
driver.find_element(:id, "div2").find_element(:name, "same").click
```

Find multiple elements

As its name suggests, `find_elements` return a list of matched elements. Its syntax is exactly
the same as `find_element`, i.e. can use any of 8 locators.

The test statements will find two checkboxes under `div#container` and click the second one.

```
checkbox_elems = driver.find_elements(:xpath, "//div[@id='container']//input\
[@type='checkbox']")
checkbox_elems.count   # => 2
checkbox_elems[1].click
```

Sometimes `find_element` fails due to multiple matching elements on a page, which you were
not aware of. `find_elements` will come in handy to find them out.

3. Hyperlink

Hyperlinks (or links) are fundamental elements of web pages. As a matter of fact, it is hyperlinks that makes the World Wide Web possible. A sample link is provided below, along with the HTML source.

Recommend Selenium

HTML Source

```
<a href="index.html" id="recommend_selenium_link" class="nav" data-id="123" \
style="font-size: 14px;">Recommend Selenium</a>
```

Click a link by text

```
driver.find_element(:link_text, "Recommend Selenium").click
```

Click a link by ID

```
driver.find_element(:id, "recommend_selenium_link").click
```

If you are testing a web site with multiple languages, using IDs is probably the only feasible option. You do not want to write test scripts like below:

```
if is_italian?
  driver.find_element(:link_text, "Accedi").click
elsif is_chinese? # a helper function determines the locale
  driver.find_element(:link_text, "登录").click
else
  driver.find_element(:link_text, "Sign in").click
end
```

Click a link by partial text

```
driver.find_element(:partial_link_text, "partial").click
expect(driver.text).to include("This is partial link page")
```

Click a link by XPath

The example below is finding a link with text 'Recommend Selenium' under a <p> tag.

```
driver.find_element(:xpath, "//p/a[text()='Recommend Selenium']").click()
```

Your might say the example before (find by :link_text) is simpler and more intuitive, that's correct. but let's examine another example:

First div Click here
Second div Click here

On this page, there are two 'Click here' links.

HTML Source

```
<div>
  First div
  <a href="link-url.html">Click here</a>
</div>
<div>
  Second div
  <a href="link-partial.html">Click here</a>
</div>
```

If a test case requires you to click the second 'Click here' link, the simple find_element(:link_text, 'Click here') won't work (as it clicks the first one). Here is a way to accomplish using XPath:

```
driver.find_element(:xpath, '//div[contains(text(), "Second")]/a[text()="Cli\
ck here"]').click()
```

Click Nth link with exact same label

It is not uncommon that there are more than one link with exactly the same text. By default, Selenium will choose the first one. What if you want to click the second or Nth one?

The web page below contains three 'Show Answer" links,

1. Do you think automated testing is important and valuable? Show Answer

2. Why didn't you do automated testing in your projects previously? Show Answer

3. Your project now has so comprehensive automated test suite, What changed? Show Answer

To click the second one,

```
driver.find_elements(:link_text => "Show Answer")[1].click # second link
```

find_elements return a list (also called array) of web controls matching the criteria in appearing order. Selenium (in fact Ruby) uses 0-based indexing, i.e., the first one is 0.

Verify a link present or not?

```
assert driver.find_element(:link_text, "Recommend Selenium").displayed?
assert !driver.find_element(:id, "recommend_selenium_link").displayed?
```

Verification in RSpec (known as RSpec Expectations):

```
# RSpec's expect-based syntax
expect(driver.find_element(:link_text, "Recommend Selenium").displayed?).to \
be_truthy
expect(driver.find_element(:link_text, "Recommend Selenium").displayed?).not\
_to be_falsey

# RSpec's should-based syntax
driver.find_element(:link_text, "Recommend Selenium").displayed?.should be_t\
ruthy
driver.find_element(:id, "recommend_selenium_link").displayed?.should_not be\
_falsey
```

The *expect*, *should*, *should_not*, *be_truthy* and *be_falsey* are defined in RSpec.

For more information, check out RSpec documentation[1].

Getting link data attributes

Once a web control is identified, we can get its other attributes of the element. This is generally applicable to most of the controls.

```
expect(driver.find_element(:link_text, "Recommend Selenium")["href"]).to eq(\
site_url.gsub("link.html", "index.html"))
expect(driver.find_element(:link_text, "Recommend Selenium")["id"]).to eq("r\
ecommend_selenium_link")
expect(driver.find_element(:id, "recommend_selenium_link").text).to eq("Reco\
mmend Selenium")
expect(driver.find_element(:id, "recommend_selenium_link").tag_name).to eq("\
a")
```

Also you can get the value of custom attributes of this element and its inline CSS style.

```
expect(driver.find_element(:id, "recommend_selenium_link").attribute("data-i\
d")).to eq("123")
expect(driver.find_element(:id, "recommend_selenium_link")["style"]).to eq("\
font-size: 14px;")
```

Test links open a new browser window

Clicking the link below will open the linked URL in a new browser window or tab.

```
<a href="http://testwisely.com/demo" target="_blank">Open new window</a>
```

While we could use switch_to method (see chapter 10) to find the new browser window, it will be easier to perform all testing within one browser window. Here is how:

---

[1]https://github.com/rspec/rspec-expectations

```
current_url = driver.current_url
new_window_url = driver.find_element(:link_text, "Open new window")["href"]
driver.navigate.to(new_window_url)
# ... testing on new site
driver.find_element(:name, "name").send_keys "sometext"
driver.navigate.to(current_url) # back
```

In this test script, we use a local variable (a programming term) 'current_url' to store the current URL.

4. Button

Buttons can come in two forms - standard and submit buttons. Standard buttons are usually created by the 'button' tag, whereas submit buttons are created by the 'input' tag (normally within form controls).

Standard button

Choose Selenium

Submit button in a form

Username: [_____] Submit

HTML Source

```
<button id="selenium_btn" class="nav" data-id="123" style="font-size: 14px;"\
>Choose Selenium</button>
<!-- ... -->
<form name="input" action="index.html" method="get">
  Username: <input type="text" name="user">
  <input type="submit" name="submit_action" value="Submit">
</form>
```

Please note that some controls look like buttons, but are actually hyperlinks by CSS styling.

Click a button by text

```
driver.find_element(:xpath, "//button[contains(text(),'Choose Selenium')]").\
click
```

Click a form button by text

For an input button (in a HTML input tag) in a form, the text shown on the button is the 'value' attribute which might contain extra spaces or invisible characters.

```
<input type="submit" name="submit_action" value="Space After "/>
```

The test script below will fail as there is a space character in the end.

```
driver.find_element(:xpath, "//input[@value='Space After']").click
```

Changing to match the value exactly will fix it.

```
driver.find_element(:xpath, "//input[@value='Space After ']").click
```

Submit a form

In the official Selenium tutorial, the operation of clicking a form submit button is done by calling *submit* function on an input element within a form. For example, the test script below is to test user sign in.

```
username_element = driver.find_element(:name, "user")
username_element.send_keys("agileway")
password_element = driver.find_element(:name, "password")
password_element.send_keys("secret")
username_element.submit
```

However, this is not my preferred approach. Whenever possible, I write test scripts this way: one test step corresponds to one user operation, such as a text entry or a mouse click. This helps me to identify issues quicker during test debugging. Using *submit* means testers need a step to define a variable to store an identified element (line 1 in above test script), to me, it breaks the flow. Here is my version:

```
driver.find_element(:name, "user").send_keys("agileway")
driver.find_element(:name, "password").send_keys("secret")
driver.find_element(:xpath, "//input[@value='Sign in']").click
```

Furthermore, if there is more than one submit button (unlikely but possible) in a form, calling *submit* is equivalent to clicking the first submit button only, which might cause confusion.

Click a button by ID

As always, a better way to identify a button is to use IDs. This applies to all controls, if there are IDs present.

```
driver.find_element(:id, "selenium_btn").click
```

 For testers who work with the development team, rather than spending hours finding a way to identify a web control, just go to programmers and ask them to add IDs. It usually takes very little effort for programmers to do so.

Click a button by name

In an input button, we can use a new generic attribute name to locate a control.

```
driver.find_element(:name, "submit_action").click
```

Click a image button

There is also another type of 'button': an image that works like a submit button in a form.

Go →

```
<input type="image" src="images/button_go.jpg"/>
```

Besides using ID, the button can also be identified by using *src* attribute.

```
driver.find_element(:xpath, "//input[contains(@src, 'button_go.jpg')]").click
```

Click a button via JavaScript

You may also invoke clicking a button via JavaScript. I had a case where normal approaches didn't click a button reliably on Firefox, but this Javascript way worked well.

```
the_btn = driver.find_element(:id, "searchBtn")
driver.execute_script("arguments[0].click();", the_btn);
```

Assert a button present

Just like hyperlinks, we can use displayed? to check whether a control is present on a web page. This check applies to most of the web controls in Selenium.

```
expect(driver.find_element(:id, "selenium_btn").displayed?).to be_truthy
driver.find_element(:link_text, "Hide").click
sleep 0.5
expect(driver.find_element(:id, "selenium_btn").displayed?).to be_falsey
```

Assert a button enabled or disabled?

A web control can be in a disabled state. A disabled button is un-clickable, and it is displayed differently.

Choose Selenium

Normally enabling or disabling buttons (or other web controls) is triggered by JavaScripts.

```
expect(driver.find_element(:id, "selenium_btn").enabled?).to be_truthy
driver.find_element(:link_text, "Disable").click
sleep 0.5
expect(driver.find_element(:id, "selenium_btn").enabled?).to be_falsey
driver.find_element(:link_text, "Enable").click
sleep 0.5
expect(driver.find_element(:id, "selenium_btn").enabled?).to be_truthy
```

5. TextField and TextArea

Text fields are commonly used in a form to pass user entered text data to the server. There are two variants (prior to HTML5): password fields and text areas. The characters in password fields are masked (shown as asterisks or circles). Text areas allows multiple lines of texts.

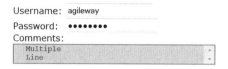

HTML Source

```
Username: <input type="text" name="username" id="user"> <br>
Password: <input type="password" name="password" id="pass"> <br/>
Comments: <br/>
<textarea id="comments" rows="2" cols="60" name="comments"></textarea>
```

Enter text into a text field by name

```
driver.find_element(:name, "username").send_keys("agileway")
```

The 'name' attribute is the identification used by the programmers to process data. It applies to all the web controls in a standard web form.

Enter text into a text field by ID

```
driver.find_element(:id, "user").send_keys("tester1")
```

Enter text into a password field

In Selenium, password text fields are treated as normal text fields, except that the entered text is masked.

```
driver.find_element(:id, "pass").send_keys("testisfun")
```

Clear a text field

Calling send_keys to the same text field will concatenate the new text with the old text. So it is a good idea to clear a text field first, then send keys to it.

```
driver.find_element(:name, "username").send_keys("test")
driver.find_element(:name, "username").send_keys(" wisely") #=> 'test wisely'
driver.find_element(:name, "username").clear
driver.find_element(:name, "username").send_keys("agileway")
```

Enter text into a multi-line text area

Selenium treats text areas the same as text fields.

```
driver.find_element(:id, "comments").send_keys("Selenium is\r\nFun!")
```

The "\r\n" represents a new line.

Assert value

```
driver.find_element(:id, "user").send_keys("testwisely")
expect(driver.find_element(:id, "user")["value"]).to eq("testwisely")
```

Focus on a control

Once we identify one control, we can set the focus on it. There is no *focus* function on *element* in Selenium, we can achieve 'focusing a control' by sending empty keystrokes to it.

```
driver.find_element(:id, "pass").send_keys("")
```

Or using JavaScript.

```
the_elem = driver.find_element(:id, "pass")
driver.execute_script("arguments[0].focus();", the_elem)
```

This workaround can be quite useful. When testing a long web page and some controls are not visible, trying to click them might throw "Element is not visible" error. In that case, setting the focus on the element might make it a visible.

Set a value to a read-only or disabled text field

'Read only' and 'disabled' text fields are not editable and are shown differently in the browser (typically grayed out).

```
Read only text field:
<input type="text" name="readonly_text" readonly="true"/> <br/>
Disabled text field:
<input type="text" name="disabled_text" disabled="true"/>
```

If a text box is set to be read-only, the following test step will not work.

```
driver.find_element(:name, "readonly_text").send_keys("new value")
```

Here is a workaround:

```
driver.execute_script("$('#readonly_text').val('bypass');")
expect(driver.find_element(:id, "readonly_text")["value"]).to eq("bypass")
driver.execute_script("$('#disabled_text').val('anyuse');")
```

The below is a screenshot of a disabled and read-only text fields that were 'injected' with two values by the above test script.

Disabled text field: anyuse
Readonly text field: bypass

Set and assert the value of a hidden field

A hidden field is often used to store a default value.

```
<input type="hidden" name="currency" value="USD"/>
```

The below test script asserts the value of the above hidden field and changes its value using JavaScript.

```
the_hidden_elem = driver.find_element(:name, "currency")
expect(the_hidden_elem["value"]).to eq("USD")
driver.execute_script("arguments[0].value = 'AUD';", the_hidden_elem)
expect(driver.find_element(:name, "currency")["value"]).to eq("AUD")
```

6. Radio button

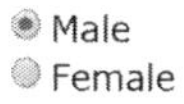

⦿ Male
◯ Female

HTML Source

```
<input type="radio" name="gender" value="male" id="radio_male" checked="true\
">Male<br>
<input type="radio" name="gender" value="female" id="radio_female">Female
```

Select a radio button

```
driver.find_element(:xpath, "//input[@name='gender' and @value='female']").c\
lick
sleep 0.5
driver.find_element(:xpath, "//input[@name='gender' and @value='male']").cli\
ck
```

The radio buttons in the same radio group have the same name. To click one radio option, the value needs to be specified. Please note that the value is not the text shown next to the radio button, that is the label. To find out the value of a radio button, inspect the HTML source.

As always, if there are IDs, using :id finder is easier.

```
driver.find_element(:id, "radio_female").click
```

Clear radio option selection

It is OK to click a radio button that is currently selected, however, it would not have any effect.

```
driver.find_element(:id, "radio_female").click
# already selected, no effect
driver.find_element(:id, "radio_female").click
```

Once a radio button is selected, you cannot just clear the selection in Selenium. (Watir, another test framework, can clear radio selection). You need to select another radio button. The test script below will throw an error: "invalid element state: Element must be user-editable in order to clear it."

```
driver.find_element(:xpath, "//input[@name='gender' and @value='female']").c\
lick

begin
  driver.find_element(:xpath, "//input[@name='gender' and @value='female']")\
.clear
rescue => e
  # Selenium does not allow
  puts "Selenium not allow clear selected radio button, select another one"
  driver.find_element(:xpath, "//input[@name='gender' and @value='male']").c\
lick
end
```

Assert a radio option is selected

The below script ensures the radio button is selected.

```
driver.find_element(:xpath, "//input[@name='gender' and @value='female']").c\
lick
expect(driver.find_element(:xpath, "//input[@name='gender' and @value='femal\
e']").selected?).to be_truthy
```

Iterate radio buttons in a radio group

So far we have been focusing on identifying web controls by using one type of locator find_-element. Here I introduce another type of locator (I call them plural locators): find_elements.

```
expect(driver.find_elements(:name => "gender").size).to eq(2)
driver.find_elements(:name => "gender").each do |rb|
  rb.click if rb["value"] == "female"
end
```

Different from `find_element` which returns one matched control, `find_elements` return a list of them (also known as an array) back. This can be quite handy especially when controls are hard to locate.

Click Nth radio button in a group

```
driver.find_elements(:name => "gender")[1].click
expect(driver.find_element(:xpath, "//input[@name='gender' and @value='femal\
e']").selected?).to be_truthy
driver.find_elements(:name => "gender")[0].click
expect(driver.find_element(:xpath, "//input[@name='gender' and @value='male'\
]").selected?).to be_truthy
```

 Once I was testing an online calendar, there were many time-slots, and the HTML for each of these time-slots were exactly the same. I simply identified the time slot by using the index (as above) on one of these 'plural' locators.

Click radio button by the following label

Some .NET controls generate poor quality HTML fragments like the one below:

```
<div id="q1" class="question">
  <div class="question-answer col-lg-5">
    <div class="yes-no">
      <input id="QuestionViewModels_1__SelectedAnswerId" name="QuestionViewM\
odels[1].SelectedAnswerId" type="radio" value="c225306e-8d8e-45b0-8261-22617\
d9796b5">
      <label for="QuestionViewModels_1__SelectedAnswerId">Yes</label>
    </div>
    <div class="yes-no">
      <input id="QuestionViewModels_1__SelectedAnswerId" name="QuestionViewM\
odels[1].SelectedAnswerId" type="radio" value="85ff8db7-1c58-47a2-a978-58120\
0fb7098">
      <label for="QuestionViewModels_1__SelectedAnswerId">No</label>
    </div>
  </div>
</div>
```

The id attribute of the above two radio buttons are the same, and the values are meaningless to human. The only thing can be used to identify a radio button is the text in label elements. The solution is to use XPath locator. You might have noticed that input (radio button) and label are siblings in the HTML DOM tree. We can use this relation to come up a XPath that identifies the label text, then the radio button.

```
elem = driver.find_element(:xpath, "//div[@id='q1']//label[contains(.,'Yes')\
]/../input[@type='radio']")
elem.click
```

Customized Radio buttons - iCheck

There are a number of plugins that customize radio buttons into a more stylish form, like the one below (using iCheck).

Gender: ✓ Male ○ Female

The iCheck JavaScript transforms the radio button HTML fragment

```
<input type="radio" name="sex" id="q2_1" value="male"> Male
```

to

```
<div class="iradio_square-red" style="position: relative;">
    <input type="radio" name="sex" id="q2_1" value="male" styl="....
    <ins class="iCheck-helper" style="...
</div>
```

Here are test scripts to drive iCheck radio buttons.

```
# Error: Element is not clickable
# driver.find_element(:id, "q2_1").click

driver.find_elements(:class, "iradio_square-red").first.click
driver.find_elements(:class, "iradio_square-red").last.click

# More precise with XPath
driver.find_element(:xpath, "//div[contains(@class, 'iradio_square-red')]/in\
put[@type='radio' and @value='male']/..").click
```

7. CheckBox

☐ I have a bike
☑ I have a car

HTML Source

```
<input type="checkbox" name="vehicle_bike" value="on" id="checkbox_bike">I h\
ave a bike<br>
<input type="checkbox" name="vehicle_car" id="checkbox_car">I have a car
```

Select by name

```
driver.find_element(:name => "vehicle_bike").click
driver.find_element(:name, "vehicle_bike").click # alternative
```

The above two test statements work identically. However, the first one allows adding more attributes such as:

```
# :index is not supported yet, just an example of showing syntax
driver.find_element(:name => "vehicle_bike", :index => 1).click
```

Clicking a checkbox, in fact, is a toggle, i.e, first click checks and the next one unchecks. The test statement below makes sure a check is a check.

```
driver.find_element(:name, "vehicle_bike").click unless driver.find_element(\
:name, "vehicle_bike").selected?
```

Uncheck a checkbox

```
the_checkbox = driver.find_element(:name => "vehicle_bike")
the_checkbox.click if the_checkbox.selected?
```

Assert a checkbox is checked (or not)

```
the_checkbox = driver.find_element(:name => "vehicle_bike")
the_checkbox.click unless the_checkbox.selected?
expect(the_checkbox.selected?).to be_truthy
the_checkbox.click
expect(the_checkbox.selected?).to be_falsey
```

Customized Checkboxes - iCheck

There are a number of plugins that customize radio buttons into a more stylish form, like the one below (using iCheck).

☐ Soccer
☑ Basketball
☐ Baseball

The iCheck JavaScript transforms the checkbox HTML fragment

```
<input type="checkbox" name="sports[]" value="Soccer">  Soccer <br/>
```

to

```
<div class="icheckbox_square-red" style="position: relative;">
   <input type="checkbox" name="sports[]" value="Soccer" style="....
   <ins class="iCheck-helper" style="...
</div>
```

Here are test scripts to drive iCheck checkboxes.

```
driver.find_elements(:class, "icheckbox_square-red").first.click # First
sleep 0.5 # add some delays for JavaScript to execute
driver.find_elements(:class, "icheckbox_square-red")[1].click   # Second
sleep 0.5
# More precise with XPath
driver.find_element(:xpath, "//div[contains(@class, 'icheckbox_square-red')]\
/input[@type='checkbox' and @value='Soccer']/..").click
```

8. Select List

A Select list is also known as a drop-down list or combobox.

Make:

HTML Source

```
<select name="car_make" id="car_make_select">
  <option value="">-- Select --</option>
  <option value="honda">Honda (Japan)</option>
  <option value="volvo">Volvo (Sweden)</option>
  <option value="audi">Audi (Germany)</option>
</select>
```

Select an option by text

The label of a select list is what we can see in the browser.

```
Selenium::WebDriver::Support::Select.new(driver.find_element(:name, "car_mak\
e")).select_by(:text, "Volvo (Sweden)")
```

Select an option by value

The value of a select list is what to be passed to the server.

```
Selenium::WebDriver::Support::Select.new(driver.find_element(:id, "car_make_\
select")).select_by(:value, "audi")
```

Select an option by iterating all options

Here I will show you a far more complex way to select an option in a select list, not for the sake of complexity, of course. A select list contains options, where each option itself is a valid control in Selenium.

```
my_select = driver.find_element(:id, "car_make_select")
my_select.find_elements( :tag_name => "option" ).find do |option|
  option.text == "Volvo (Sweden)"
end.click
```

Select multiple options

A select list also supports multiple selections.

Framework:

HTML Source

```
<select id="framework_select" name="test_framework" multiple="multiple">
  <option></option>
  <option value="rwebspec">RWebSpec</option>
  <option value="watir">Watir</option>
  <option value="selenium">Selenium</option>
</select>
```

```
select_box = Selenium::WebDriver::Support::Select.new(driver.find_element(:n\
ame, "test_framework"))
select_box.select_by(:text, "Selenium")
select_box.select_by(:text, "RWebSpec")
```

Clear one selection

```
select_box = Selenium::WebDriver::Support::Select.new(driver.find_element(:n\
ame, "test_framework"))
select_box.select_by(:text, "Selenium")
select_box.select_by(:value, "rwebspec")
select_box.deselect_by(:text, "RWebSpec") # by label
select_box.deselect_by(:index, 3) # :index
# now no options are selected
```

Clear selection

Clear selection works the same way for both single and multiple select lists.

```
select_box = Selenium::WebDriver::Support::Select.new(driver.find_element(:n\
ame, "test_framework"))
select_box.deselect_all
```

Assert selected option

To verify a particular option is currently selected in a select list:

```
my_select =  Selenium::WebDriver::Support::Select.new(driver.find_element(:i\
d, "car_make_select"))
my_select.select_by(:value, "audi")
expect(my_select.first_selected_option.text).to eq("Audi (Germany)")

# However, cannot use value for assertion
# expect(my_select.first_selected_option.value).to eq("audi")
```

Assert the value of a select list

Another quick (and simple) way to check the current selected value of a select list:

```
my_select = Selenium::WebDriver::Support::Select.new(driver.find_element(:na\
me, "car_make"))
my_select.select_by(:text, "Volvo (Sweden)")
expect(my_select.first_selected_option["value"]).to eq("volvo")
```

Assert multiple selections

A multiple select list can have multiple options being selected.

```
my_select = Selenium::WebDriver::Support::Select.new(driver.find_element(:na\
me, "test_framework"))

my_select.select_by(:text, "Selenium")
my_select.select_by(:text, "RWebSpec")

selected = my_select.selected_options
expect(selected.size).to eq(2)
expect(selected[0].text).to eq("RWebSpec") # based on displaying order
expect(selected[1].text).to eq("Selenium")
```

Please note, even though the test script selected 'Selenium' first, when it comes to assertion, the first selected option is 'RWebSpec', not 'Selenium'.

9. Navigation and Browser

Driving common web controls were covered from chapters 2 to 7. In this chapter, I will show how to manage browser windows and page navigation in them.

Go to a URL

```
driver.get("http://testwisely.com");
driver.navigate.to("https://testwisely.com/demo")
```

Visit pages within a site

driver.navigate.to takes a full URL. Most of time, testers test against a single site and specifying a full URL (such as http://...) is not necessary. We can create a reusable function to simplify its usage.

```
$site_root_url = "http://test.testwisely.com" # test server

# ...

def visit(path)
  driver.navigate.to("#{$site_root_url}#{path}")
end

it "Go to page within the site" do
  visit("/demo")
  visit("/demo/survey")
  visit("/")  # home page
end
```

Apart from being more readable, there is another benefit with this approach. If you want to run the same test against at a different server (the same application deployed on another machine), we only need to make one change: the value of $site_root_url.

```
$site_root_url = "http://staging.testwisely.com" # another server
# ...
```

Perform actions from right mouse click context menu such as 'Back', 'Forward' or 'Refresh'

Operations with right click context menu are commonly page navigations, such as "Back to previous page". We can achieve the same by calling the test framework's navigation operations directly.

```
driver.navigate.back
driver.navigate.refresh
driver.navigate.forward
```

Open browser in certain size

Many modern web sites use responsive web design, that is, page content layout changes depending on the browser window size. Yes, this increases testing effort, which means testers need to test web sites in different browser window sizes. Fortunately, Selenium has a convenient way to resize the browser window.

```
driver.manage().window().resize_to(1024, 768)
```

Maximize browser window

```
driver.manage().window().maximize
sleep 1 # wait 1 second to see the effect
driver.manage().window().resize_to(1280, 800)
```

Move browser window

We can move the browser window (started by the test script) to a certain position on screen, (0, 0) is the top left of the screen. The position of the browser's window won't affect the test results. This might be useful for utility applications, for example, a background video program can capture a certain area on screen.

```
driver.manage().window().move_to(100, 200)
sleep 1
driver.manage().window().move_to(0, 0)
```

Minimize browser window

Surprisingly, there is no `minimize` window function in Selenium. The hack below achieves the same:

```
driver.manage().window().move_to(-2000, 0)
sleep 1
driver.manage().window().move_to(0, 0)
```

While the browser's window is minimized, the test execution still can run.

Scroll focus to control

For certain controls are not viewable in a web page (due to JavaScript), WebDriver unables to click on them by returning an error like *"Element is not clickable at point (1180, 43)"*. The solution is to scroll the browser view to the control.

```
elem = driver.find_element(:name, "submit_action_2")
elem_pos = elem.location.y
driver.execute_script("window.scroll(0, #{elem_pos})")
```

Switch between browser windows or tabs

A "`target='_blank'`" hyperlink opens a page in another browser window or tab (depending on the browser setting). Selenium drives the browser within a scope of one browser window. However, we can use Selenium's `switch_to` function to change the target browser window.

```
driver.find_element(:link_text, "Open new window").click # target='_blank' l\
ink
driver.switch_to.window(driver.window_handles[-1]) # switch to the last tab
expect(driver.find_element(:tag_name => "body").text).to include("This is ur\
l link page")
driver.switch_to.window(driver.window_handles[0]) # back to first tab
expect(driver.find_element(:link_text, "Open new window").displayed?).to be_\
truthy
```

Remember current web page URL, then come back to it later

We can store the page's URL into an instance variable (@url, for example).

```
before(:each) do
  # ...
  @url = driver.current_url
end

it "Go to other pages then go back directly to remembered URL" do
  driver.find_element(:link, "Button").click
  # ...
  driver.navigate.to(@url)
end
```

In previous recipes, I used local variables to remember some value, and use it later. Some might ask why "@" in the front of url? That's because a local variable only works in its local scope, typically within one test case (in our context, or more specifically between it "..." do to end).

In this example, the url variable is defined in before(:each) scope. To make it accessible to the test cases in the test script file, I define it as an instance variable @url.

10. Assertion

Without assertions (or often known as checks), a test script is incomplete. Common assertions for testing web applications are:

- page title (equals)
- page text (contains or does not contain)
- page source (contains or does not contain)
- input element value (equals)
- display element text (equals)
- element state (selected, disabled, displayed)

Assert page title

```
expect(driver.title).to eq("TestWise IDE")   # RSpec expect-syntax
driver.title.should == "TestWise IDE" # RSpec should-syntax
```

Assert Page Text

Example web page

```
Text assertion with a   (tab before), and
(new line before)!
```

HTML source

```
<PRE>Text assertion with a  (<b>tab</b> before), and
(new line before)!</PRE>
```

Test script

```
matching_str = "Text assertion with a  (tab before), and \n(new line before)\
!"
expect(driver.find_element(:tag_name => "body").text).to include(matching_st\
r)
```

Please note the `find_element(:tag_name => "body").text` returns the text view of a web page after stripping off the HTML tags, but may not be exactly the same as we saw on the browser.

Assert Page Source

The page source is raw HTML returned from the server.

```
matching_html = "Text assertion with a  (<b>tab</b> before), and \n(new line\
 before)!"
expect(driver.page_source).to include(matching_html)
```

Assert Label Text

HTML source

```
<label id="receipt_number">NB123454</label>
```

Label tags are commonly used in web pages to wrap some text. It can be quite useful to assert a specific text.

```
expect(driver.find_element(:id, "label_1").text).to eq("First Label")
```

Assert Span text

HTML source

```
<span id="span_2">Second Span</span>
```

From testing perspectives, spans are the same as labels, just with a different tag name.

```
expect(driver.find_element(:id, "span_2").text).to eq("Second Span")
```

Assert Div text or HTML

Example page

Wise Products
TestWise
BuildWise

HTML source

```
<div id="div_parent">
   Wise Products
   <div id="div_child_1">
          TestWise
   </div>
   <div id="div_child_2">
          BuildWise
   </div>
 </div>
```

Test script

```
expect(driver.find_element(:id, "div_child_1").text).to eq("TestWise")
expect(driver.find_element(:id, "div_parent").text).to eq("Wise Products\nTe\
stWise\nBuildWise")
```

The below checks for the HTML fragment of an element.

```
elem = driver.find_element(:id, "div_parent")
elem_html = driver.execute_script("return arguments[0].outerHTML;", elem)
expect(the_element_html.strip).to eq('<div id="div_parent">
 Wise Products
 <div id="div_child_1">
   TestWise
 </div>
 <div id="div_child_2">
   BuildWise
 </div>
</div>')
```

Assert Table text

HTML tables are commonly used for displaying grid data on web pages.

Example page

A	B
a	b

HTML source

```
<table id="aha_table" cellpadding="1" border="1" width="30%">
  <tr id="row_1">
    <td id="cell_1_1">A</td>
    <td id="cell_1_2">B</td>
  </tr>
  <tr id="row_2">
    <td id="cell_2_1">a</td>
    <td id="cell_2_2">b</td>
  </tr>
</table>
```

Test script

```
elem = driver.find_element(:id, "alpha_table")
expect(elem.text).to eq("A B\na b")
elem_html = driver.execute_script("return arguments[0].outerHTML;", elem_htm\
l)
expect(elem_html).to include("<td id=\"cell_1_1\">A</td>")
```

Assert text in a table cell

If a table cell (td tag) has a unique ID, it is easy.

```
expect(driver.find_element(:id, "cell_1_1").text).to eq("A")
```

An alternative approach is to identify a table cell using row and column indexes (both starting with 1).

```
expect(driver.find_element(:xpath, "//table/tbody/tr[2]/td[2]").text).to eq(\
"b")
```

Assert text in a table row

```
expect(driver.find_element(:id, "row_1").text).to eq("A B")
```

Assert image present

```
expect(driver.find_element(:id, "next_go").displayed?).to be_truthy
```

11. Frames

HTML Frames are treated as independent pages, which is not a good web design practice. As a result, few new sites use frames nowadays. However, there a quite a number of sites that uses iframes.

Testing Frames

Here is a layout of a fairly common frame setup: navigations on the top, menus on the left and the main content on the right.

HTML Source

```
<frameset rows="100,*" frameborder="0" border="0" framespacing="0">
  <frame name="topNav" src="top_nav.html">
  <frameset cols="200,*" frameborder="0" border="0" framespacing="0">
    <frame name="menu" id="menu_frame" src="menu_1.html" marginheight="0" ma\
rginwidth="0" scrolling="auto" noresize>
    <frame name="content" src="content.html" marginheight="0" marginwidth="0\
" scrolling="auto" noresize>
  </frameset>
</frameset>
```

To test a frame with Selenium, we need to identify the frame first by ID or NAME, and then switch the focus on it. The test steps after will be executed in the context of selected frame. Use `switch_to.default_content()` to get back to the page (which contains frames).

```
driver.switch_to.frame("topNav") # frame name
driver.find_element(:link_text, "Menu 2 in top frame").click

# need to switch to default before another switch
driver.switch_to.default_content()
driver.switch_to.frame("menu_frame") # frame id
driver.find_element(:link_text, "Green Page").click

driver.switch_to.default_content()
driver.switch_to.frame("content")
driver.find_element(:link_text, "Back to original page").click
```

This script clicks a link in each of three frames: top, left menu and content.

Testing IFrame

An iframe (Inline Frame) is an HTML document embedded inside another HTML document on a web site.

Example page

Enter name: [   ]

Username: [   ]
Password: [   ]
[Login]

☐ I accept terms and conditions

HTML Source

```
<IFRAME frameborder='1' id="Frame1" src="login_iframe.html"
        Style="HEIGHT: 100px; WIDTH: 320px; MARGIN=0" SCROLLING="no" >
</IFRAME>
```

The test script below enters text in the main page, fills the sign in form in an iframe, and ticks the checkbox on the main page:

```
driver.navigate.to(site_url.gsub("index.html", "iframe.html"))
driver.find_element(:name, "user").send_keys("agileway")
driver.switch_to.frame("Frame1")
driver.find_element(:name, "username").send_keys("tester")
driver.find_element(:name, "password").send_keys("TestWise")
driver.find_element(:id, "loginBtn").click
expect(driver.page_source).to include("Signed in")
driver.switch_to.default_content()
driver.find_element(:id, "accept_terms").click
```

The web page after test execution looks as below:

Please note that the content of the iframe changed, but not the main page.

Test multiple iframes

A web page may contain multiple iframes.

```
driver.switch_to.frame(0)
driver.find_element(:name, "username").send_keys("agileway")
driver.switch_to.default_content()
driver.switch_to.frame(1)
driver.find_element(:id, "radio_male").click
```

12. Testing AJAX

AJAX (an acronym for Asynchronous JavaScript and XML) is widely used in web sites nowadays (Gmail uses AJAX a lot). Let's look at an example first:

On clicking 'Transfer' button, an animated loading image showed up indicating 'transfer in progress'.

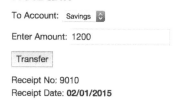

After the server processing the request, the loading image is gone and a receipt number is displayed.

From testing perspective, a test step (like clicking 'Transfer' button) is completed immediately. However the updates to parts of a web page may happen after unknown delay, which differs from traditional web requests.

There are 2 common ways to test AJAX operations: waiting enough time or checking the web page periodically for a maximum given time.

Wait within a time frame

After triggering an AJAX operation (clicking a link or button, for example), we can set a timer in our test script to wait for all the asynchronous updates to occur before executing next step.

```
driver.find_element(:xpath,"//input[@value='Transfer']").click
sleep 10
expect(driver.find_element(:tag_name => "body").text).to include("Receipt No\
:")
```

`sleep 10` means waiting for 10 seconds, after clicking 'Transfer' button. 10 seconds later, the test script will check for the 'Receipt No:' text on the page. If the text is present, the test passes; otherwise, the test fails. In other words, if the server finishes the processing and return the results correctly in 11 seconds, this test execution would be marked as 'failed'.

Explicit Waits until Time out

Apparently, the waiting for a specified time is not ideal. If the operation finishes earlier, the test execution would still be on halt. Instead of passively waiting, we can write test scripts to define a wait statement for certain condition to be satisfied until the wait reaches its timeout period. If Selenium can find the element before the defined timeout value, the code execution will continue to next line of code.

```
driver.find_element(:xpath,"//input[@value='Transfer']").click
wait = Selenium::WebDriver::Wait.new(:timeout => 10) # seconds
wait.until{ driver.find_element(:id => "receiptNo").text.to_i > 0 }
```

Implicit Waits until Time out

An implicit wait is to tell Selenium to poll finding a web element (or elements) for a certain amount of time if they are not immediately available. The default setting is 0. Once set, the implicit wait is set for the life of the WebDriver object instance, until its next set.

```
driver.find_element(:id, "rcptAmount").send_keys("250")
driver.find_element(:xpath,"//input[@value='Transfer']").click
driver.manage.timeouts.implicit_wait = 10 # seconds
expect(driver.find_element(:id => "receiptNo").text.to_i).to be > 0
driver.manage.timeouts.implicit_wait = 0  # don't wait any more
```

Create your own polling check function

The Explicit Waits and Implicit Waits in Selenium can be used to handle AJAX operation well. Here I want to show another rudimentary solution from different perspective.

```
driver.find_element(:id, "transfer_btn").click # AJAX

timeout = 10     # can change
start_time = Time.now
last_error = nil
until (duration = Time.now - start_time) > timeout
  begin
    expect(driver.page_source).to include("Receipt No:")  # the check
    last_error = nil
    break;
  rescue => e
    last_error = e
  end
  sleep 1 # polling interval
end
```

Refactor with a reusable function

The above test script works, but is hard to read. We can refactor it by extracting this common functionality into a reusable function: try_for.

```
def try_for(timeout = 30, polling_interval = 1, &block)
  start_time = Time.now

  last_error = nil
  until (duration = Time.now - start_time) > timeout
    begin
      yield
      last_error = nil
      return true
    rescue => e
      last_error = e
    end
    sleep polling_interval
  end

  raise "Timeout after #{duration.to_i} seconds with error: #{last_error}." \
if last_error
```

```
  raise "Timeout after #{duration.to_i} seconds."
end
```

(If you feel confused, don't worry. This function is already included in the sample tests scripts. If you follow the convention used in this book, you only need to know how to use it.)

Our test script is now like this:

```
# includes a helper containing try_for method

it "AJAX Call function to try periodically" do
  ...
  driver.find_element(:xpath,"//input[@value='Transfer']").click
  try_for(10) { expect(driver.find_element(:tag_name => "body").text).to inc\
lude("Receipt No:") }
end
```

Much better, isn't it? The syntax for using try_for is as below:

```
  AJAX_OPERATION
  try_for(SECONDS) { NEXT_TEST_STATEMENT }
```

We can use try_for for all kinds of AJAX operations.

Wait AJAX Call to complete using JQuery

If the target application uses JQuery for Ajax requests (most do), you may use a JavaScript call to check active Ajax requests: jQuery.active is a variable JQuery uses internally to track the number of simultaneous AJAX requests.

1. drive the control to initiate AJAX call
2. wait until the value of jQuery.active is zero
3. continue the next operation

The *waiting* is typically implemented in a reusable function.

```ruby
it "test with AJAX Call" do
  # ...
  driver.find_element(:xpath,"//input[@value='Pay now']").click
  wait_for_ajax_complete(10)
  expect(page_text).to include("Booking number")
end

def wait_for_ajax_complete(max_seconds)
  max_seconds.times do
    is_ajax_complete = driver.execute_script("return jQuery.active == 0")
    if is_ajax_complete
      return
    end
    sleep(1)
  end
  raise "Timed out waiting for AJAX call after #{max_seconds} seconds"
end
```

13. File Upload and Popup dialogs

In this chapter, I will show you how to handle file upload and popup dialogs. Most of pop up dialogs, such as 'Choose File to upload', are native windows rather than browser windows. This would be a challenge for testing as Selenium only drives browsers. If one pop up window is not handled properly, test execution will be on halt.

File upload

Example page

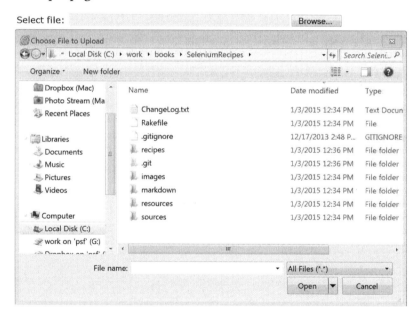

HTML Source

```
<input type="file" name="document[file]" id="files" size="60"/>
```

Test script

```
driver.find_element(:name, "document[file]").send_keys("C:\\testdata\\logo.p\
ng"))
```

The first slash of \\ is for escaping the later one, the whole purpose is to pass the value "C:\testdata\logo.png" to the control.

Some might say, hard coding a file path is not a good practice. It's right, it is generally better to include your test data files within your test project, then use relative paths to refer to them, as the example below:

```
selected_file = File.join(File.dirname(__FILE__), "testdata", "users.csv")
selected_file = selected_file.gsub("/", "\\") # for on windows
driver.find_element(:name, "document[file]").send_keys(selected_file)
```

In Ruby, the path separator is '/', the second statement in the above test script is to convert it to the windows path separator.

JavaScript pop ups

JavaScript pop ups are created using javascript, commonly used for confirmation or alerting users.

There are many discussions on handling JavaScript Pop ups in forums and Wikis. I tried several approaches. Here I list two stable ones:

Handle JavaScript pop ups using Alert API

```
driver.find_element(:xpath, "//input[contains(@value, 'Buy Now')]").click
a = driver.switch_to.alert
# debug a.text
if a.text == 'Are you sure?'
  a.accept
else
  a.dismiss
end
```

Handle JavaScript pop ups with JavaScript

```
driver.execute_script "window.confirm = function() { return true; }"
driver.execute_script "window.alert = function() { return true; }"
driver.execute_script "window.prompt = function() { return true; }"
driver.find_element(:id, "buy_now_btn").click
```

Different from the previous approach, the pop up dialog is not even shown.

This recipe is courtesy of Alister Scott's WatirMelon blog[1]

Modal style dialogs

Flexible Javascript libraries, such as Bootstrap Modals[2], replace the default JavaScript alert dialogs used in modern web sites. Strictly speaking, a modal dialog like the one below is not a pop-up.

Comparing to the raw JS *alert*, writing automated tests against modal popups is easier.

---

[1]http://watirmelon.com/2010/10/31/dismissing-pesky-javascript-dialogs-with-watir/
[2]http://getbootstrap.com/javascript/#modals

```
driver.find_element(:id, "bootbox_popup").click
sleep 0.5
driver.find_element(:xpath, "//div[@class='modal-footer']/button[text()='OK'\
]").click
```

Bypass basic authentication by embedding username and password in URL

Authentication dialogs, like the one below, can be troublesome for automated testing.

A very simple way to get pass Basic or NTLM authentication dialogs: prefix username and password in the URL.

```
driver = Selenium::WebDriver.for :firefox
driver.navigate.to "http://tony:password@itest2.com/svn-demo/"
# got in, click a link
driver.find_element(:link_text, "tony/").click
```

Timeout on an operation

When a pop up window is not handled, it blocks the test execution. This is worse than a test failure when running a number of test cases. For operations that are prone to hold ups, we can add a time out with a specified maximum time.

```
require 'timeout'
Timeout::timeout(5) {
  driver.alert.ok
}
```

Internet Explorer modal dialog

Modal dialog, only supported in Internet Explorer, is a dialog (with 'Webpage dialog' suffix in title) that user has to deal with before interacting with the main web page. It is considered as a bad practice, and it is rarely found in modern web sites. However, some unfortunate testers might have to deal with modal dialogs.

Example page

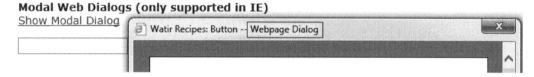

HTML Source

```
<a href="javascript:void(0);" onclick="window.showModalDialog('button.html')\
">Show Modal Dialog</a>
```

Test script

```
driver.find_element(:link, "Show Modal Dialog").click
driver.switch_to.window(driver.window_handles[-1]) # switch to modal win
driver.find_element(:name, "user").send_keys("in_modal")
driver.switch_to.window(driver.window_handles[0])  # switch to main win
driver.find_element(:name, "status").send_keys("done")
```

Popup Handler Approach

There are other types of pop ups too, such as Basic Authentication and Security warning dialogs. How to handle them? The fundamental difficulty behind pop up dialog handling is that some of these dialogs are native windows, not part of the browser, which means they are beyond the testing library's (i.e. Selenium) control.

Here I introduce a generic approach to handle all sorts of pop up dialogs. Set up a monitoring process (let's call it popup handler) waiting for notifications of possible new pop ups. Once the popup hander receives one, it will try to handle the pop up dialog with data received using windows automation technologies. It works like this:

```
#  . . .
NOTIFY_HANDLER_ABOUT_TO_TRIGGER_A_POPUP_OPERATION
PERFORM_OPERATION
#  . . .
```

BuildWise Agent[3] is a tool for executing automated tests on multiple machines in parallel. It has a free utility named 'Popup handler' just does that.

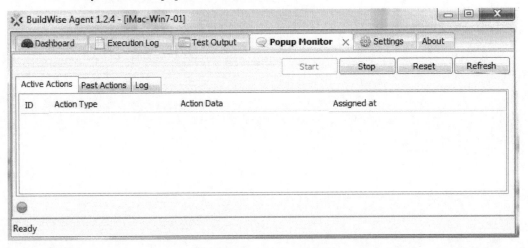

Handle JavaScript dialog with Popup Handler

---

[3]http://testwisely.com/buildwise

```
# this will click 'OK' in popup window
handle_popup(:popup) {
  driver.find_element(:xpath, "//input[contains(@value, 'Buy Now')]").click
}
```

The handle_popup is a function defined in *popup_handler_helper.rb*, which is included in the same project.

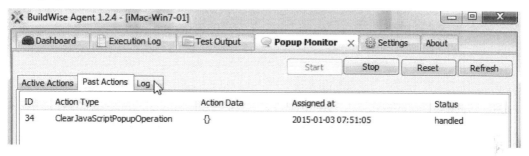

Basic or Proxy Authentication Dialog

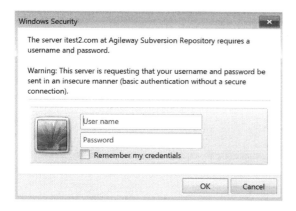

```
handle_popup(:basic_auth,
    { :username => "tony", :password => "password",
      :win_title => "Connect to"}) {
  driver.get("http://itest2.com/svn-demo/")
}
driver.find_element(:link_text, "tony/").click
```

The same test steps can also be applied to proxy authentication dialogs.

14. Debugging Test Scripts

Debugging usually means analyzing and removing bugs in the code. In the context of automated functional testing, debugging is to find out why a test step did not execute as expected and fix it.

Print text for debugging

```
puts "Now on page: " + driver.title
app_no = driver.find_element(:id, "app_id").text
puts "Application number is " + app_no
```

Here is the output from executing the above test from command line:

```
Now on page: Assertion Test Page
Application number is 1234
```

When the test is executed in a Continuous Integration server, output is normally captured and shown. This can be quite helpful on debugging test execution.

Write text to IDE output

When developing test scripts in an IDE, it might be convenient to write debugging text to an output window in IDE for easy viewing. But be warned that the test script must still run just fine outside the tool.

The below test script writes the output to TestWise console window using debug function.

```
debug driver.title
app_no = driver.find_element(:id, "app_id").text
debug "Application number is " + app_no
```

```
23    ⊟    it "Write text to TestWise console" do
24            debug browser.title
25            app_no = browser.find_element(:id, "app_id").text
26            debug "Application number is " + app_no
```

```
Console
Assertion Test Page
 25: app_no = browser.find_element(:id, "app_id").text
Application number is 1234
```

One important matter is that adding this convenience shall not sacrifice the independence of test scripts. That is, the test scripts shall run fine from command line.

Write page source or element HTML into a file

When the text you want to inspect is large (such as the page source), printing out the text to a console will not be helpful (too much text). A better approach is to write the output to a temporary file and inspect it later. It is often a better way to write to a temporary file, and use some other tool to inspect later.

```
File.open("c:\\temp\\login_page.html", "w").write(driver.page_source);
```

You can also just dump a specific part of web page:

```
elem = driver.find_element(:id, "div_parent")
elem_html = driver.execute_script("return arguments[0].outerHTML;", elem)
File.open("c:\\temp\\login_parent.xhtml", "w").write(elem_html);
```

Take screenshot

Taking a screenshot of the current browser window when an error/failure happened is a good debugging technique. Selenium supports it in a very easy way.

```
driver.save_screenshot("C:\\temp\\screenshot.png")
```

The above works. However, when it is run the second time, it will return error "The file already exists". A simple workaround is to write a file with timestamped file name, as below:

```
# save to timestamped file, e.g. screenshot-04071544.png
driver.save_screenshot("C:\\screenshot-#{Time.now.strftime('%m%d%H%M')}.png")
```

Some test IDEs, such as TestWise, has a feature to auto capture screenshots when errors occurred. These screenshots are often included in a test report.

Here is a sample test report containing a screenshot of web page when an error occurred.

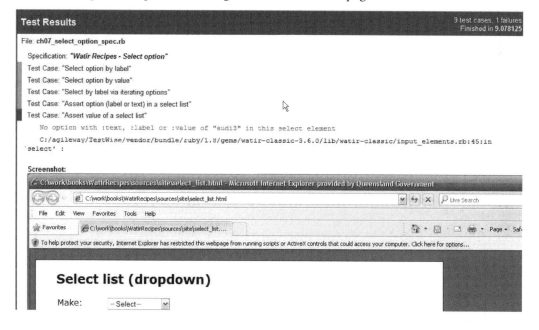

Using IRB

Interactive Ruby (IRB, it comes with Ruby distribution) lets users enter Ruby programs interactively and see the results immediately.

```
> irb
irb(main):001:0> require 'selenium-webdriver'
=> true
irb(main):002:0> driver = Selenium::WebDriver.for(:firefox)
=> #<Selenium::WebDriver::Driver:0x44ee643c browser=:firefox>
irb(main):003:0> driver.navigate.to("http://testwisely.com/demo")
=> ""
irb(main):004:0> driver.find_element(:link, "NetBank").click
=> "ok"
```

Leave browser open after test finishes

Once an error or failure occurred during test execution, a tester's immediate instinct is to check two things: which test statement is failed on and what current web page is like. The first one can be easily found in the testing tools (or command line output). We need the browser to stay open to see the web page. However, we don't want that when running a group of tests, as it will affect the execution of the following test cases.

All of our sample test scripts listed in this book have this:

```
after(:all) do
  driver.close unless debugging?
end
```

That unless debugging? tells TestWise to leave the browser open only when running individual test case. When running multiple test cases, this statement is ignored by TestWise, i.e., the browser will be closed to get ready to run the next test case.

Pause/Stop test execution at certain step

Pause, Stop and Run to line are typical debugging features in programming IDEs. If your testing IDE supports them (TestWise Professional edition does, as the screenshot below) and you are comfortable of using them (some are over complicated for debugging test scripts), that's good.

```
it "User failed to sign in due to invalid password" do
  @browser.find_element(:id, "username").send_keys("agileway")
  @browser.find_element(:id, "password").send_keys("badpass")
  @browser.find_element(:id, "username").submit
  @browser.page_source.include?("Invalid email o
end
```

Icon	Menu Item
▷≣	Run "User failed to sign in due to inva..."
▷	Run test cases in 'login_spec.rb'
	Run Selected Scripts Against Current Browser
	Run to this line

If not, here I show an extremely simple way: adding a long sleep.

```
#...
sleep 10
#...
```

Once the test execution is on halt, you can do inspection against the web page. Or you can event stop the test execution. Some may say "This is not good, I don't want to mess up with my test scripts with some sleep statements". It is a fair comment. Back to basics, do what you think appropriate to get the job done.

Run selected test steps against current browser

One feature I miss most from Watir in Selenium is the ability to attach execution to an existing browser window. This is a very useful feature for debugging tests. When a test step fails, after analyzing and/or modifying (the test scripts or application), we often would like to rerun the test case continuing from where it stopped, rather than starting from the beginning again.

One solution is to create a temporary test script file with selected test steps, following a test statement which can attach to the current browser window. Some readers might wonder: you said browser attaching is not supported in Selenium, bear with me for a moment.

```
# temporary test file
load File.dirname(__FILE__) + '/test_helper.rb'
describe "Selenium Recipes - CheckBox" do
  include TestHelper

  it "Selected" do
    use_current_browser
    # run one or several steps directly against the current browser, yeah!
    driver.find_element(:name, "vehicle_car").click
  end
end
```

It is a good idea to keep this temporary test script file in the same folder as the main test scripts, so that it can reference to other dependent files, *test_helper* for example.

How does use_current_browser work? It uses $browser, a global variable, which stores the browser window instance lastly used.

```
before(:all) do
  @driver = $driver = Selenium::WebDriver.for(browser_type)
end
```

However, this approach only works when executing tests within in parent process, such as an IDE. The 'Run selected test scripts' feature in TestWise Professional Edition works just this way.

```
29    it "User failed to sign in due to invalid password" do
30      @browser.find_element(:id, "username").send_keys("agileway")
31      @browser.find_element(:id, "password").send_keys("b      ")
32      @browser.find_element(:id, "username").submit        Run "User failed to sign in due to inva..."
33      @browser.page_source.include?("Invalid email or pas   Run test cases in 'login_spec.rb'
34    end                                                     Run Selected Scripts Against Current Browser
35
```

15. Test Data

Gathering test data is an important but often neglected activity. Thanks to the power and flexibility of Ruby, testers now have a new ability to prepare test data.

Get date dynamically

```ruby
require 'date' # only need to require once
# assume today is 2014-10-25
Date.today.strftime("%m/%d/%Y")  # => 10/25/2014
(Time.now + 1 * 24 * 3600).strftime("%Y-%m-%d %H:%M") # => 2014-10-26 12:24
```

Based on the above, we can create easy to read date related functions (see the helper method in the sample project), like the one below

```ruby
# default to UK/AUS date format
def today(date_format = "%d/%m/%Y")
  date_format = "%m/%d/%Y" if date_format.to_s == "us"
  Date.today.strftime(date_format)
end
```

Then you can use the following in your test scripts.

```ruby
today               #=> 25/10/2014
today(:us)          #=> 10/26/2014
today("%Y-%m-%d")   #=> 2014-10-26
```

rwebspec_utils.rb (included in recipe source zip file, available on the book site[1]) contains a set of date related helper methods:

---

[1]http://zhimin.com/books/selenium-recipes

```
yesterday          # 24/10/2014
tomorrow           # 26/10/2014
days_from_now(3)   # 29/10/2014
days_before(3)     # 23/10/2014
```

Example use

```
expect(driver.find_element(:id, "date").text).to eq(today)
```

Get a random boolean value

A boolean value means either *true* or *false*. Getting a random true or false might not sound that interesting. That was what I thought when I first learned it. Later, I realized that it is actually very powerful, because I can fill the computer program (test script as well) with nondeterministic data.

```
rand(2) == 1 # true or false
```

For example, in a user sign up form, we could write two cases: one for male and one for female. With random boolean, I could achieve the same with just one test case. If the test case get run many times, it will cover both scenarios.

```
driver.find_element(:xpath, "//input[@type='radio' and @name='gender' and @v\
alue='#{random_value}']").click
```

Generate a number within a range

```
rand(10)      # a random number 0 up to 9, different each run
rand(90) + 10 # a number between 10 and 99
```

The test statement below will enter a number between 16 to 96. If the test gets run hundreds of times, not a problem at all for an automated test, it will cover driver's input for all permitted ages.

```
driver.find_element(:id, "drivers_age").send_keys(rand(80) + 16)
```

Get a random character

```
# random_number() can be found in rwebspec_utils.rb in book source
def random_number(min, max)
  rand(max-min+1)+min
end

random_number(97, 122).chr # lower case, a..z
random_number(65, 90).chr  # up case, A..Z
```

Get a random string at fixed length

```
# generate 10 characters lower case string
10.times.inject([]) { |str, el| str << random_number(97, 122).chr }.join
```

The above statement is quite complex. By creating some utility functions (you can find in source project), we can get quite readable test scripts as below:

```
debug random_str(7) #  example: "dolorem"
debug words(5) #  example: "sit doloremque consequatur accusantium aut"
debug sentences(3)
debug paragraphs(2)
```

Get a random string in a collection

```
def random_string_in(arr)
  return nil if arr.empty?
  index = random_number(0, arr.length-1)
  arr[index]
end


random_string_in(["Yes", "No", "Maybe"])   # one of these strings
```

I frequently use this in my test scripts.

Generate random person names, emails, addresses with Faker

Faker[2] is a Ruby library that generates fake data.

```
require 'faker'
Faker::Name.name                    # => "Jeromy Erdman"
Faker::Name.first_name              # => "Alexandre"
Faker::Internet.email               # => "justine_wolf@ryan.com"
Faker::Address.street_address       # => "290 Nienow Flats"
Faker::PhoneNumber.phone_number     # => "(206)223-6173"
```

You can find more examples at Faker[3] web site. By default, addresses and phone numbers are US format, however, you can switch to another locale or add customization[4].

Generate a test file at fixed sizes

When testing file uploads, testers often try test files in different sizes. The following ruby statement generates a test file in precise size on the fly.

---

[2]https://github.com/stympy/faker
[3]https://github.com/stympy/faker
[4]https://github.com/stympy/faker#customization

```
File.open(File.join(File.dirname(__FILE__), "tmp", "2MB.txt"), "w") {|f|
  f.write( '0' * 1024 * 1024 * 2 )
}
```

Retrieve data from Database

The ultimate way to obtain accurate test data is to retrieve from the database. For many projects, this might not be possible. For ones do, this provides the ultimate flexibility in terms of getting test data.

The test script example below is to enter the oldest (by age) user's login into the text field on a web page. To get this oldest user in the system, I use SQL to query the database directly (SQLite3 in this example, it will be different for yours, but the concept is the same).

```
require 'sqlite3'
db = SQLite3::Database.new File.join(File.dirname(__FILE__), "..", "testdata\
", "sample.db")

# Users table: with login, name, age
oldest_user_login = nil
db.execute( "select * from users order by age desc" ) do |row|
  oldest_user_login = row[0]
  break
end

expect(oldest_user_login).to eq("mark")
driver.navigate.to(site_url.gsub("index.html", "text_field.html"))
driver.find_element(:id, "user").send_keys oldest_user_login
```

16. Browser Profile and Capabilities

Selenium can start browser instances with various profile preferences which can be quite useful. Obviously, some preference settings are browser specific, so you might take some time to explore. In this chapter, I will cover some common usage.

Get browser type and version

Detecting browser type and version is useful to write custom test scripts for different browsers.

```ruby
driver = Selenium::WebDriver.for(:chrome)
puts driver.capabilities.browser_name # => chrome
puts driver.capabilities.platform # => mac os x
puts driver.capabilities.version # => 33.0.1750.152
driver.quit


driver = Selenium::WebDriver.for(:firefox)
driver.capabilities.browser_name.should == "firefox"
if RUBY_PLATFORM =~ /darwin/
  expect(driver.capabilities.platform).to eq(:darwin) # mac
elsif RUBY_PLATFORM =~ /mingw/
  # old versions may return :winnt
  expect(driver.capabilities.platform).to eq(:windows)
end


driver = Selenium::WebDriver.for(:ie)
driver.capabilities.browser_name          # "internet explorer"
```

Set HTTP Proxy for Browser

Here is an example to set HTTP proxy server for Firefox browser.

```
profile = Selenium::WebDriver::Firefox::Profile.new
profile['network.proxy.type'] = 1
# See http://kb.mozillazine.org/Network.proxy.type

profile['network.proxy.http'] = "myproxy.com"
profile['network.proxy.http_port'] = 3128
driver = Selenium::WebDriver.for :firefox, :profile => profile
driver.navigate.to "http://testwisely.com/demo"
```

Verify file download in Chrome

To efficiently verify a file is downloaded, we would like to

- save the file to a specific folder
- avoid "Open with or Save File" dialog

```
# Change default download directory, /Users/YOU/Downloads on Mac
download_path = RUBY_PLATFORM =~ /mingw/ ? "C:\\TEMP": "/Users/zhimin/tmp"
prefs = {
  :download => {
    :prompt_for_download => false,
    :default_directory => download_path
  }
}
driver = Selenium::WebDriver.for :chrome, :prefs => prefs
driver.navigate.to "http://zhimin.com/books/pwta"
driver.find_element(:link_text, "Download").click
sleep 10 # wait download to complete
expect(File.exists?("#{download_path}/practical-web-test-automation-sample.p\
df")).to be_truthy
```

This is the new way (from v2.37) to pass preferences to Chrome.

More Chrome preferences: http://src.chromium.org/svn/trunk/src/chrome/common/pref_-names.cc[1]

---

[1]http://src.chromium.org/svn/trunk/src/chrome/common/pref_names.cc

Test downloading PDF in Firefox

```
download_path = RUBY_PLATFORM =~ /mingw/ ? "C:\\TEMP": "/Users/zhimin/tmp"
profile = Selenium::WebDriver::Firefox::Profile.new
profile["browser.download.folderList"] = 2
profile["browser.download.dir"] = download_path
profile["browser.helperApps.neverAsk.saveToDisk"] = 'application/pdf'
# disable Firefox's built-in PDF viewer
profile["pdfjs.disabled"] = true

driver = Selenium::WebDriver.for :firefox, :profile => profile
driver.navigate.to "http://zhimin.com/books/selenium-recipes"
driver.find_element(:link_text, "Download").click
sleep 10 # wait download to complete
expect(File.exists?("#{download_path}/practical-web-test-automation-sample.p\
df")).to be_truthy
```

Bypass basic authentication with Firefox AutoAuth plugin

There is another complex but quite useful approach to bypass basic authentication: use a browser extension. Take Firefox for example, "Auto Login"[2] submits HTTP authentication dialogs remembered passwords.

By default, Selenium starts Firefox with an empty profile, which means no remembered passwords and extensions. We can instruct Selenium to start Firefox with an existing profile.

- Start Firefox with a dedicated profile. Run the command below (from command line)
  Windows:

  ```
  "C:\Program Files (x86)\Mozilla Firefox\firefox.exe" -p
  ```

  Mac:

---

[2]https://addons.mozilla.org/en-US/firefox/addon/autoauth/

```
/Applications/Firefox.app/Contents/MacOS/firefox-bin  -p
```

- Create a profile (I name it 'testing') and start Firefox with this profile

- Install autoauth plugin. A simple way: drag the file *autoauth-2.1-fx+fn.xpi* (included with the test project) to Firefox window.

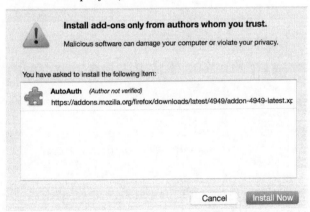

- Visit the web site requires authentication. Manually type the user name and password. Click 'Remember Password'.

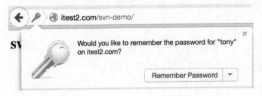

Now the preparation work is done (and only need to be done once).

```
# Prerequisite: the password is already remembered in 'testing' profile.
profile = Selenium::WebDriver::Firefox::Profile.from_name 'testing'
profile.add_extension File.join(File.dirname(__FILE__), '..', 'autoauth-2.1-\
fx+fn.xpi')
driver = Selenium::WebDriver.for :firefox, :profile => profile
driver.navigate.to "http://itest2.com/svn-demo/"
driver.find_element(:link_text, "tony/").click
```

The 'testing' profile name must be supplied, otherwise it won't work.

Manage Cookies

```
driver.get("http://travel.agileway.net")
driver.manage.add_cookie(:name => "username", :value => "natalie" )
driver.manage.all_cookies.each do |a_cookie|
  # ...
end
driver.manage.cookie_named("username")[:value] # => "natalie"
```

Headless browser testing with PhantomJS

A headless browser is a web browser without a graphical user interface. The main benefit of headless browser testing is performance. PhantomJS[3] is a headless browser that built on top of WebKit, the engine behind both Safari and Chrome. First of all, you need download phantomjs.exe, start

```
C:\>phantomjs --webdriver=2816
[INFO  - 2015-11-05T22:35:01.183Z] GhostDriver - Main - running on port 2816
```

---

[3]http://phantomjs.org/

```
driver = Selenium::WebDriver.for(:remote, :url => "http://localhost:2816")
driver.get("http://travel.agileway.net")
expect(driver.title).to eq("Agile Travel")
driver.quit
```

If your target application is relatively stable and not using JavaScript heavily, and you want gain test faster execution time, PhantomJS is a viable option.

Frankly, I am not big fan of headless browser testing for the reasons below:

- It is NOT a real browser.
- I need inspect the web page when a test failed, I cannot do that with PhantomJS. In test automation, as we know, we perform this all the time.
- To achieve faster execution time, I prefer distributing tests to multiple build agents to rum them in parallel as a part of Continuous Testing process. That way, I get not only much faster execution time (throwing in more machines), also get useful features such as quick feedback, rerunning failed tests on another build agent, dynamic execution ordering by priority, etc. All in real browsers.

Test responsive websites

Modern websites embrace responsive design to fit in different screen resolutions on various devices, such as iPad and smartphones. Bootstrap is a very popular responsive framework. How to verify your web site's responsiveness is a big question, it depends what you want to test. A quick answer is to use WebDriver's driver.manage().window().resize_to to set your browser to a target resolution, and then execute tests.

The example below verify a text box's width changes when switching from a desktop computer to a iPad, basically, whether responsive is enabled or not..

```
driver.manage().window().resize_to(1024, 768) # Desktop
driver.get("https://support.agileway.net")
width_desktop = driver.find_element(:name, "email").size.width
driver.manage().window().resize_to(768, 1024) # iPad
width_ipad = driver.find_element(:name, "email").size.width
expect(width_desktop).to be < width_ipad    # 960 vs 358
```

17. Advanced User Interactions

The ActionBuilder in Selenium WebDriver provides a way to set up and perform complex user interactions. Specifically, grouping a series of keyboard and mouse operations and sending to the browser.

Mouse interactions

- click
- click_and_hold
- context_click
- double_click
- drag_and_drop
- drag_and_drop_by
- move_by
- move_to
- release

Keyboard interactions

- key_down
- key_up
- send_keys

The usage

`driver.action.` + one or more above operations + `.perform`

Check out the ActionBuilder API[1] for more.

Double click a control

---

[1]http://selenium.googlecode.com/git/docs/api/rb/Selenium/WebDriver/ActionBuilder.html

```
elem = driver.find_element(:id, "pass")
driver.action.double_click(elem).perform
```

Move mouse to a control - Mouse Over

```
elem = driver.find_element(:id, "email")
driver.action.move_to(elem).perform
```

Click and hold - select multiple items

The test scripts below click and hold to select three controls in a grid.

```
driver.navigate.to("http://jqueryui.com/selectable")
driver.find_element(:link_text, "Display as grid").click
sleep 0.5
driver.switch_to.frame(0)
list_items = driver.find_elements(:xpath, "//ol[@id='selectable']/li")
driver.action.click_and_hold(list_items[1]).click_and_hold(list_items[3]).cl\
ick.perform
driver.switch_to.default_content
```

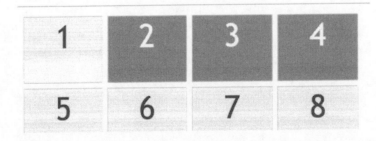

Context Click - right click a control

```
driver.navigate.to(site_url.gsub("index.html", "text_field.html"))
sleep 0.5
elem = driver.find_element(:id, "pass")
# browser specific, the scripts below does 'paste' in Firefox
if driver.capabilities.browser_name == "firefox"
  driver.action.context_click(elem)
                .send_keys(:down)
                .send_keys(:down)
                .send_keys(:down)
                .send_keys(:down)
                .send_keys(:return)
                .perform
end
```

Drag and drop

Drag-n-drop is increasingly common in new web sites. Testing this feature can be largely achieved in Selenium WebDriver, I used the word 'largely' which means achieving the same outcome, but not the 'mouse dragging' part. In this example page,

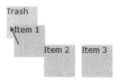

the test script below will *drop* 'Item 1' to 'Trash'.

```
drag_from = driver.find_element(:id, "item_1")
target = driver.find_element(:id, "trash")
driver.action.drag_and_drop(drag_from, target).perform
```

The below is a screenshot after the test execution.

Drag slider

Slider (a part of JQuery UI library) provide users an very intuitive way to adjust values (typically in settings).

The test below simulates 'dragging the slider to the right'.

```
expect(driver.find_element(:id, "pass_rate").text).to eq("15%")
elem = driver.find_element(:id, "pass-rate-slider")
driver.action.drag_and_drop_by(elem, 2, 0).perform
expect(driver.find_element(:id, "pass_rate").text).not_to eq("15%")
```

More information about `drag_and_drop_by` can be found at Selenium ActionBuild Ruby API[2].

The below is a screenshot after the test execution.

Please note that the percentage figure after executing the test above are always 50% (I saw 49% now and then).

Send key sequences - Select All and Delete

---

[2]http://selenium.googlecode.com/git/docs/api/rb/Selenium/WebDriver/ActionBuilder.html#drag_and_drop_by-instance_method

```
driver.find_element(:id, "comments").send_keys("Multiple Line\r\n Text")
elem = driver.find_element(:id, "comments")
driver.action.click(elem)
            .key_down(:control)
            .send_keys("a")
            .key_up(:control)
            .perform
driver.action.send_keys(:backspace).perform
```

Please note that the last test statement is different from `elem.send_keys`. The keystrokes triggered by `action.send_keys` is sent to the active browser window, not a specific element.

18. HTML 5 and JavaScript

Web technologies are evolving. HTML5 includes many new features for more dynamic web applications and interfaces. Furthermore, wide use of JavaScript (thanks to popular JavaScript libraries such as JQuery), web sites nowadays are much more dynamic. In this chapter, I will show some Selenium examples to test HTML5 elements and interactive operations with JavaScript.

Please note that some tests only work on certain browsers (Chrome is your best bet), as some HTML5 features are not fully supported in some browsers yet.

HTML5 Email type field

Let's start with a simple one. An email type field is used for input fields that should contain an e-mail address. From the testing point of view, we treat it exactly the same as a normal text field.

Email field

> jam

HTML Source

```
<input id="email" name="email" type="email" style="height:30px; width: 280px\
;">
```

```
driver.find_element(:id, "email").send_keys("test@wisely.com")
```

HTML5 Time Field

The HTML5 time field is much more complex, as you can see from the screenshot below.

Time

> 08:27 am ⊗ ↕

HTML Source

```
<input id="start_time_1" name="start_time" type="time" style="height:30px; w\
idth: 120px;">
```

The test scripts below do the following:

1. make sure the focus is not on this time field control
2. click and focus the time field
3. clear existing time
4. enter a new time

```
# focus on another control ...
driver.find_element(:id, "home_link").send_keys("")
sleep 0.5

# now back to change it
driver.find_element(:id, "start_time_1").click
driver.find_element(:id, "start_time_1").send_keys([:delete, :left, :delete,\
 :left, :delete])

driver.find_element(:id, "start_time_1").send_keys("08")
sleep 0.3
driver.find_element(:id, "start_time_1").send_keys("27")
sleep 0.3
driver.find_element(:id, "start_time_1").send_keys("AM")
```

Invoke 'onclick' JavaScript event

In the example below, when user clicks on the text field control, the tip text (*'Max 20 characters'*) is shown.

Example page

| | Max 20 characters |

HTML Source

```
<input type="text" name="person_name" onclick="$('#tip').show();" onchange=\
"change_person_name(this.value);"/>
<span id="tip" style="display:none; margin-left: 20px; color:gray;">Max 20 c\
haracters</span>
```

When we use normal `send_keys` in Selenium, it enters the text OK, but the tip text is not displayed.

```
driver.find_element(:name, "person_name").send_keys "Wise Tester"
```

We can simply call 'click' to achieve it.

```
driver.find_element(:name, "person_name").clear
driver.find_element(:name, "person_name").send_keys "Wise Tester"
driver.find_element(:name, "person_name").click
expect(driver.find_element(:id, "tip").text).to eq("Max 20 characters")
```

Invoke JavaScript events such as 'onchange'

A generic way to invoke 'OnXXXX' events is to execute JavaScript, the below is an example to invoke 'OnChange' event on a text box.

```
driver.find_element(:id, "person_name_textbox").send_keys "Test Wise"
driver.execute_script("$('#person_name_textbox').trigger('change')");
expect(driver.find_element(:id, "person_name_label").text).to eq("Test Wise")
```

Scroll to the bottom of a page

Calling JavaScript API.

```
driver.execute_script("window.scrollTo(0, document.body.scrollHeight);")
```

Or send the keyboard command: 'Ctrl+End'.

```
driver.action.key_down(:control).send_keys(:end).key_up(:control).perform
```

Chosen - Standard Select

Chosen is a popular JQuery plug-in that makes long select lists more user-friendly, it turns the standard HTML select list box into this:

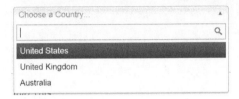

HTML Source

```
<select id="chosen_single" class="chosen-select"  data-placeholder="Choose a\
 Country..." style="width:350px;">
  <option value=""></option>
  <option value="United States">United States</option>
  <option value="United Kingdom">United Kingdom</option>
  <option value="Australia">Australia</option>
</select>
```

The HTML source seems not much different from the standard select list excepting adding the class chosen-select. By using the class as the identification, the JavaScript included on the page generates the following HTML fragment (beneath the select element).

Generated HTML Source

```
<div class="chosen-container chosen-container-single chosen-container-active\
" style="width: 350px;" title="" id="chosen_single_chosen">
  <a class="chosen-single chosen-default" tabindex="-1"><span>Choose a Count\
ry...</span><div><b></b></div></a>
  <div class="chosen-drop">
    <div class="chosen-search">
      <input type="text" autocomplete="off" tabindex="2">
    </div>
    <ul class="chosen-results">
```

```
      <li class="active-result" style="" data-option-array-index="1">United \
States</li>
      <li class="active-result result-selected" style="" data-option-array-i\
ndex="2">United Kingdom</li>
      <li class="active-result" style="" data-option-array-index="3">Austral\
ia</li>
    </ul>
  </div>
</div>
```

Please note that this dynamically generated HTML fragment is not viewable by 'View Page Source', you need to enable the inspection tool (usually right mouse click the page, then choose 'Inspect Element') to see it.

Before we test it, we need to understand how we use it.

- Click the 'Choose a Country'
- Select an option

There is no difference from the standard select list. That's correct, we need to understand how Chosen emulates the standard select list first. In Chosen, clicking the 'Choose a Country' is actually clicking a hyper link with class "chosen-single" under the div with ID "chosen_single_chosen" (the ID is whatever set in the select element, followed by '_chosen'); selecting an option is clicking an list item (tag: li) with class 'active-result'. With that knowledge, plus XPath in Selenium, we can drive a Chosen standard select box with the test scripts below:

```
sleep 2 # wait enough time to load JS
driver.find_element(:xpath, "//div[@id='chosen_single_chosen']//a[contains(@\
class,'chosen-single')]").click
available_items = driver.find_elements(:xpath, "//div[@id='chosen_single_cho\
sen']//div[@class='chosen-drop']//li[contains(@class,'active-result')]")
available_items.select{|x| x.text == "Australia"}.first.click

sleep 1
driver.find_element(:xpath, "//div[@id='chosen_single_chosen']//a[contains(@\
class,'chosen-single')]").click
```

```
available_items = driver.find_elements(:xpath, "//div[@id='chosen_single_cho\
sen']//div[@class='chosen-drop']//li[contains(@class,'active-result')]")
available_items.select{|x| x.text == "United States"}.first.click
```

A neat feature of Chosen is allowing user to search the option list, to do that in Selenium:

```
sleep 1
driver.find_element(:xpath, "//div[@id='chosen_single_chosen']//a[contains(@\
class,'chosen-single')]").click

search_text_field = driver.find_element(:xpath, "//div[@id='chosen_single_ch\
osen']//div[@class='chosen-drop']//div[contains(@class,'chosen-search')]/inp\
ut")
search_text_field.send_keys("United King")
sleep 0.5 # let filtering finishing
# select first selected option
search_text_field.send_keys(:enter)
```

Chosen - Multiple Select

Chosen[1] also enhances the multiple selection (a lot).

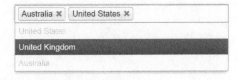

HTML Source

---

[1]http://harvesthq.github.io/chosen/

```html
<select id="chosen_multiple" class="chosen-select" multiple data-placeholder\
="Choose a Country..."  style="width:350px;">
  <option value=""></option>
  <option value="United States">United States</option>
  <option value="United Kingdom">United Kingdom</option>
  <option value="Australia">Australia</option>
</select>
```

Again, the only difference from the standard multiple select list is the class 'chosen-select'.

Generated HTML Source

```html
<div class="chosen-container chosen-container-multi chosen-container-active"\
 style="width: 350px;" title="" id="chosen_multiple_chosen">
  <ul class="chosen-choices">
    <li class="search-choice"><span>Australia</span><a class="search-choice-\
close" data-option-array-index="3"></a></li>
    <li class="search-choice"><span>United States</span><a class="search-cho\
ice-close" data-option-array-index="1"></a></li>
    <li class="search-field"><input type="text" value="Choose a Country..." \
class="" autocomplete="off" style="width: 25px;" tabindex="4"></li>
  </ul>
  <div class="chosen-drop">
    <ul class="chosen-results">
      <li class="result-selected" style="" data-option-array-index="1">Unite\
d States</li>
      <li class="active-result" style="" data-option-array-index="2">United \
Kingdom</li>
      <li class="result-selected" style="" data-option-array-index="3">Austr\
alia</li>
    </ul>
  </div>
</div>
```

Astute readers will find the generated HTML fragment is quite different from the standard (single) select, that's because of the usage. The concept of working out driving the control is the same, I will leave the homework to you, just show the test scripts.

```ruby
sleep 2 # wait the JS to load fully
# click the box then select one option
driver.find_element(:xpath, "//div[@id='chosen_multiple_chosen']//li[@class=\
'search-field']/input").click
available_items = driver.find_elements(:xpath, "//div[@id='chosen_multiple_c\
hosen']//div[@class='chosen-drop']//li[contains(@class,'active-result')]")
available_items.select{|x| x.text == "Australia"}.first.click


# select another
driver.find_element(:xpath, "//div[@id='chosen_multiple_chosen']//li[@class=\
'search-field']/input").click
available_items = driver.find_elements(:xpath, "//div[@id='chosen_multiple_c\
hosen']//div[@class='chosen-drop']//li[contains(@class,'active-result')]")
available_items.select{|x| x.text == "United Kingdom"}.first.click
```

To deselect an option is to click the little 'x' on the right. In fact, it is the idea to clear all selections first then select the wanted options.

```ruby
# clear all selections
sleep 0.5
close_btns = driver.find_elements(:xpath, "//div[@id='chosen_multiple_chosen\
']//ul[@class='chosen-choices']/li[contains(@class,'search-choice')]/a[conta\
ins(@class,'search-choice-close')]")
close_btns.each do |cb|
  cb.click
end

driver.find_element(:xpath, "//div[@id='chosen_multiple_chosen']//li[@class=\
'search-field']/input").click
available_items = driver.find_elements(:xpath, "//div[@id='chosen_multiple_c\
hosen']//div[@class='chosen-drop']//li[contains(@class,'active-result')]")
available_items.select{|x| x.text == "United States"}.first.click
```

Some might say the test scripts are quite complex. That's good thinking, if many of our test steps are written like this, it will be quite hard to maintain. One common way is to extract them into reusable functions, like below:

```ruby
def clear_chosen(chosen_select_id)
  sleep 0.5
  close_btns = driver.find_elements(:xpath, "//div[@id='#{chosen_select_id}'\
]//ul[@class='chosen-choices']/li[contains(@class,'search-choice')]/a[contai\
ns(@class,'search-choice-close')]")
  close_btns.each do |cb|
    cb.click
  end
end



def select_chosen_label(chosen_select_id, option_label)
  driver.find_element(:xpath, "//div[@id='#{chosen_select_id}']//li[@class='\
search-field']/input").click
  available_items = driver.find_elements(:xpath, "//div[@id='#{chosen_select\
_id}']//div[@class='chosen-drop']//li[contains(@class,'active-result')]")
  available_items.select{|x| x.text == option_label}.first.click
end

# ...

it "Wrap chosen in reusable functions" do
  # ... land to the page with a chosen select list
  sleep 1

  clear_chosen("chosen_multiple_chosen")
  select_chosen_label("chosen_multiple_chosen", "United States")
  select_chosen_label("chosen_multiple_chosen", "Australia")
end
```

You can find more techniques for writing maintainable tests from my other book *Practical Web Test Automation*[2].

---

[2]https://leanpub.com/practical-web-test-automation

AngularJS web pages

AngularJS is a popular client-side JavaScript framework that can be used to extend HTML. Here is a web page (simple TODO list) developed in AngularJS.

1 of 3 remaining [archive]

- ☑ learn angular
- ☐ build an angular app
- ☑ Learn test automation

[add new todo here] [add]

HTML Source

The page source (via "View Page Source" in browser) is different from what you saw on the page. It contains some kind of dynamic coding (*ng-xxx*).

```
<div ng-controller="TodoCtrl">
  <span>{{remaining()}} of {{todos.length}} remaining</span>
  [ <a href="" ng-click="archive()">archive</a> ]
  <ul class="unstyled">
    <li ng-repeat="todo in todos">
      <input type="checkbox" ng-model="todo.done">
      <span class="done-{{todo.done}}">{{todo.text}}</span>
    </li>
  </ul>
  <form ng-submit="addTodo()">
    <input type="text" ng-model="todoText"  size="30"
           placeholder="add new todo here">
    <input class="btn-primary" type="submit" value="add">
  </form>
</div>
```

As a tester, we don't need to worry about AngularJS programming logic in the page source. To view rendered page source, which matters for testing, inspect the page via right mouse click page and select "Inspect Element".

Browser inspect view

Astute readers will notice that the 'name' attribute are missing in the input elements, replaced with 'ng-model' instead. We can use xpath to identify the web element.

The tests script below

- Add a new todo item in a text field
- Click add button
- Uncheck the 3rd todo item

```
expect(driver.page_source).to include("1 of 2 remaining")
driver.find_element(:xpath, "//input[@ng-model='todoText']").send_keys("Lear\
n test automation")
driver.find_element(:xpath, "//input[@type = 'submit' and @value='add']").cl\
ick
sleep 0.5
driver.find_elements(:xpath, "//input[@type = 'checkbox' and @ng-model='todo\
.done']")[2].click
sleep 1
expect(driver.page_source).to include("1 of 3 remaining")
```

Ember JS web pages

Ember JS is another JavaScript web framework, like Angular JS, the 'Page Source' view (from browser) of a web page is raw source code, which is not useful for testing.

HTML Source

```html
<div class="control-group">
  <label class="control-label" for="longitude">Longitude</label>
  <div class="controls">
    {{view Ember.TextField valueBinding="longitude"}}
  </div>
</div>
```

Browser inspect view

```
▼ <div class="control-group">
    ::before
    <label class="control-label" for="longitude">Longitude</label>
  ▼ <div class="controls">
      <input id="ember412" class="ember-view ember-text-field" type="text">
    </div>
    ::after
  </div>
```

The ID attribute of a Ember JS generated element (by default) changes. For example, this text field ID is "ember412".

Longitude

```
input#ember412.ember-view.ember-text-field 220px × 30px
```

Refresh the page, the ID changed to a different value.

Longitude

```
input#ember469.ember-view.ember-text-field 220px × 30px
```

So we shall use another way to identify the element.

```
ember_text_fields = driver.find_elements(:xpath, "//div[@class='controls']/i\
nput[@class='ember-view ember-text-field']")
ember_text_fields[0].send_keys("-24.0034583945")
ember_text_fields[1].send_keys("146.903459345")
ember_text_fields[2].send_keys("90%")

driver.find_element(:xpath, "//button[text() ='Update record']").click
```

"Share Location" with Firefox

HTML5 Geolocation API can obtain a user's position. By using Geolocation API, programmers can develop web applications to provide location-aware services, such as locating the nearest restaurants. When a web page wants to use a user's location information, the user is presented with a pop up for permission.

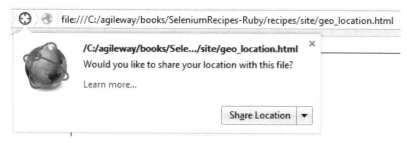

This is a native popup window, which means Selenium WebDriver cannot drive it. However, there is a workaround. We can set up a browser profile that pre-allows "Share Location" for specific websites. Here are the steps for Firefox.

1. Open Firefox with a specific profile for testing
2. Open the site
3. Type about:permissions in the address
4. Select the site and choose "Allow" option for "Share Location"

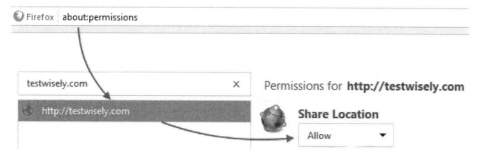

The set up and use of a specific testing profile for Firefox is already covered in Chapter 16. This only needs to be done once. After that, the test script can test location-aware web pages.

```
profile = Selenium::WebDriver::Firefox::Profile.from_name 'testing'
@driver = $browser = Selenium::WebDriver.for(:firefox, :profile => profile)
driver.find_element(:id, "use_current_location_btn").click
try_for(10) { expect(driver.find_element(:id, "demo").text).to include("Lati\
tude:")  }
```

Faking Geolocation with JavaScript

With Geolocation testing, it is almost certain that we will need to test the users in different locations. This can be done by JavaScript.

```
lati   = -34.915379  # set geo location for user
longti = 138.576777
driver.execute_script("window.navigator.geolocation.getCurrentPosition=funct\
ion(success){;  var position = {'coords' : {'latitude': '#{lati}','longitude\
': '#{longti}'}}; success(position);}");
driver.find_element(:id, "use_current_location_btn").click
try_for(10) { expect(driver.find_element(:id, "demo").text).to include("-34.\
915379")  }
```

19. WYSIWYG HTML editors

WYSIWYG (an acronym for "What You See Is What You Get") HTML editors are widely used in web applications as embedded text editor nowadays. In this chapter, we will use Selenium WebDriver to test several popular WYSIWYG HTML editors.

TinyMCE

TinyMCE is a web-based WYSIWYG editor, it claims "the most used WYSIWYG editor in the world, it is used by millions"[1].

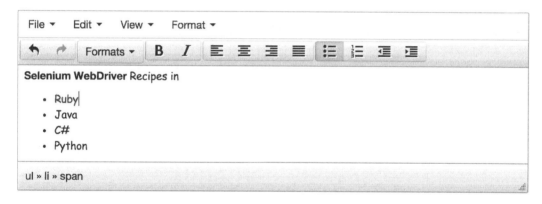

The rich text is rendered inside an inline frame within TinyMCE. To test it, we need to "switch to" that frame.

---

[1]http://www.tinymce.com/enterprise/using.php

```
@driver.navigate.to(site_url.gsub("index.html", "tinymce-4.1.9/tinyice_demo.\
html"))
sleep 1 # wait JavaScript to load
driver.switch_to.frame('mce_0_ifr')
editor_body = driver.find_element(:css => 'body')
driver.execute_script("arguments[0].innerHTML = '<h1>Heading</h1>AgileWay'",\
 editor_body)
sleep 1
editor_body.send_keys("New content")
sleep 1
editor_body.clear

driver.execute_script("arguments[0].innerHTML = '<p>one</p><p>two</p>'", edi\
tor_body)

# switch out then can drive controls on the main page
driver.switch_to.default_content
# click TinyMCE editor's 'Numbered List' button
tinymce_btn_numbered_list = driver.find_element(:css => ".mce-btn[aria-label\
='Numbered list'] button")
tinymce_btn_numbered_list.click

# Insert text calling JavaScript
driver.execute_script("tinyMCE.activeEditor.insertContent('<p>Brisbane</p>')\
")
```

CKEditor

CKEditor is another popular WYSIWYG editor. Like TinyMCE, CKEditor uses an inline frame.

```
driver.get(site_url.gsub("index.html", "ckeditor-4.4.7/samples/uicolor.html"\
))
sleep 1 # wait JS to load
ckeditor_frame = driver.find_element(:class, "cke_wysiwyg_frame")
driver.switch_to.frame(ckeditor_frame)
editor_body = driver.find_element(:tag_name, "body")
editor_body.send_keys("Selenium Recipes\n by Zhimin Zhan")
sleep 1

# Clear content Another Method Using ActionBuilder to clear()
driver.action.click(editor_body).key_down(:control).send_keys("a").key_up(:c\
ontrol).perform
driver.action.send_keys(:backspace).perform

driver.switch_to.default_content()
# click a editing button
driver.find_element(:class, "cke_button__numberedlist").click() # numbered l\
ist
```

SummerNote

SummerNote is a Bootstrap based lightweight WYSIWYG editor, different from TinyMCE or CKEditor, it does not use frames.

Selenium WebDriver Recipes in

- Ruby
- Java
- C#
- Python|

```
driver.get(site_url.gsub("index.html", "summernote-0.6.3/demo.html"))
sleep 0.5
driver.find_element(:xpath, "//div[@class='note-editor']/div[@class='note-ed\
itable']").send_keys("Text")
# click a format button: unordered list
driver.find_element(:xpath, "//button[@data-event='insertUnorderedList']").c\
lick()
# switch to code view
driver.find_element(:xpath, "//button[@data-event='codeview']").click()
# insert text to code editor
driver.find_element(:xpath, "//textarea[@class='note-codable']").send_keys("\
\n<p>HTML</p>")
```

CodeMirror

CodeMirror is a versatile text editor implemented in JavaScript. CodeMirror is not a
WYSIWYG editor, but it is often used with one for editing raw HTML source for the rich
text content.

```
1  <!-- write some xml below -->
2  <Selenium-WebDriverRecipes>
3    <book>in Ruby</book>
4    <book>in Java</book>
5    <book>in C#</book>
6    <book>in Python</book>
7  </
     </Selenium-WebDriverRecipes>
```

```ruby
@driver.navigate.to(site_url.gsub("index.html", "codemirror-5.1/demo/xmlcomp\
lete.html"))
elem = driver.find_element(:class, "CodeMirror-scroll")
elem.click
sleep 0.5
# elem.send_keys does not work
driver.action.send_keys("<A>").perform
```

20. Leverage Programming

The reason that Selenium WebDriver quickly overtakes other commercial testing tools (typically promoting record-n-playback), in my opinion, is embracing the programming, which offers the flexibility needed for maintainable automated test scripts.

In the chapter, I will show some examples that use some programming practices to help our testing needs.

Raise exceptions to fail test

While RSpec Expectation or MiniTest framework provides most of assertions needed, raising exceptions can be useful too as shown below.

```
raise "Unsupported platform #{RUBY_PLATFORM}" unless RUBY_PLATFORM.include?(\
"darwin")
```

In test output (when running on Windows):

```
Unsupported platform i386-mingw32
# ./spec/ch20_programming_spec.rb: ...
```

An exception means an anomalous or exceptional condition occurred. The code to handle exceptions is called exception handling, an important concept in programming. If an exception is not handled, the program execution will terminate with the exception displayed.

Here is anther more complete example.

```
begin
  driver =  Selenium::WebDriver.for(:chrome)
  # ...
rescue => e
  puts "Exception occurred: #{e}, #{e.backtrace}"
ensure
  driver.quit
end
```

rescue block handles the exception. If an exception is handled, the program (in our case, test execution) continues. e.backtrace returns the stack trace of the exception occurred. ensure block is always run (after) no matter exceptions are thrown (from begin) or not.

I often use exceptions in my test scripts for non-assertion purposes too.

1. Flag incomplete tests

    The problem with "TODO" comments is that you might forget them.

    ```
    it "next test" do
      # TODO
    end
    ```

    I like this way better.

    ```
    it "next test" do
      raise "TO BE DONE"
    end
    ```

2. Stop test execution during debugging a test

    Sometimes, you want to utlize automated tests to get you to a certain page in the application quickly.

    ```
    # test steps ...
    raise "Stop here, I take over from now. I delete this later."
    ```

Ignorable test statement error

When a test step can not be performed correctly, execution terminates and the test is marked as failed. However, failed to run certain test steps sometimes is OK. For example, we want to make sure a test starts with no active user session. If a user is currently signed in, try signing out; If a user has already signed out, performing signing out will fail the test, but it is acceptable.

Here is an example to capture the error/failure in a test statement (in Ruby), and then ignore:

```ruby
begin
  driver.find_element(:link, "Sign out").click
rescue => e
  # ignore
end
```

This seems quite complex. As usual, we can extract it into a reusable function:

```ruby
# try operation, ignore if errors occur
def fail_safe(& block)
  begin
    yield
  rescue =>e
  end
end
```

Now You can do this in below one-line statement:

```ruby
fail_safe{ driver.find_element(:link, "Sign out").click }
```

Read external file

We can use Ruby's built-in file I/O (input and output) functions to read data, typically test data, from external files. Try to avoid referencing an external file using absolute path like below:

```
input_file = "C:\\temp\\in.xml" # Bad
content = File.read(input_file)
# ...
```

If this test script is copied to another machine, it might fail. A common practice is to put test data with the test scripts, and refer to them using a relative path.

```
input_file = File.join(File.dirname(__FILE__), "testdata", "in.xml")
File.exists?(input_file).should == true
content = File.read(input_file)
```

Data-Driven Tests with Excel

Data-Driven Testing means a test's input are driven from external sources, quite commonly in Excel or CSV files. For instance, if there is a list of user credentials with different roles and the login process is the same (but with different assertions), you can extract the test data from an excel spreadsheet and execute it one by one. Because our test scripts are in fact Ruby scripts, it is quite easy to do so.

A sample spreadsheet (*users.xls*) contains three username-password combination:

DESCRIPTION	LOGIN	PASSWORD	EXPECTED_TEXT
Valid Login	agileway	test	Login successful!
User name not exists	notexists	smartass	Login is not valid
Password not match	agileway	badpass	Password is not valid

The test scripts below reads the above and uses the login data to drive the browser to perform tests.

```
require 'spreadsheet'
require 'selenium-webdriver'

driver = Selenium::WebDriver.for(:firefox)

# Load Excel file
excel_file = File.join(File.dirname(__FILE__), "testdata", "users.xls")
excel_book = Spreadsheet.open excel_file
sheet1 = excel_book.worksheet(0) # first sheet
```

```
# Iterate each row in the first sheet
sheet1.each_with_index do |row, idx|
  next if idx == 0 # ignore first row
  description, login, password, expected_text = row[0], row[1], row[2], row[\
3]
  driver.navigate.to("http://travel.agileway.net")
  driver.find_element(:name, "username").send_keys(login)
  driver.find_element(:name, "password").send_keys(password)
  driver.find_element(:name, "username").submit
  expect(driver.find_element(:tag_name => "body").text).to include(expected_\
text)
  # if logged in OK, try log out, so next one can continue
  fail_safe{ driver.find_element(:link_text, "Sign off").click }
end
```

(The above test script requires spreadsheet gem to be installed)

Data-Driven Tests with CSV

A CSV (comma-separated values) file stores tabular data in plain-text form. CSV files are commonly used for importing into or exporting from applications. Comparing to Excel spreadsheets, a CSV file is a text file that contains only the pure data, not formatting.

The below is the CSV version of data driving test for the above user sign in example:

```
require 'csv'
csv_file = File.join(File.dirname(__FILE__), "testdata", "users.csv")
CSV.foreach(csv_file) do |row|
  # get user login details row by row
  login, password, expected_text = row[1], row[2], row[3]
  next if login == "LOGIN" # ignore first row
  driver.navigate.to("http://travel.agileway.net")
  driver.find_element(:name, "username").send_keys(login)
  driver.find_element(:name, "password").send_keys(password)
  driver.find_element(:name, "username").submit
  # debug expected_text
```

```
expect(driver.find_element(:tag_name => "body").text).to include(expected_\
text)
  # if logged in OK, try log out, so next one can continue
  fail_safe{ driver.find_element(:link_text, "Sign off").click }
end
```

Identify element IDs with dynamically generated long prefixes

You can use regular expression to identify the static part of element ID or NAME. The below is a HTML fragment for a text box, we could tell some part of ID or NAME are machine generated (which might be different for next build), and the part "AppName" is meaningful.

```
<input id="ctl00_m_g_dcb0d043_e7f0_4128_99c6_71c113f45dd8_ctl00_tAppName_I"
  name="ctl00$m$g_dcb0d043_e7f0_4128_99c6_71c113f45dd8$ctl00$tAppName"/>
```

If we can later verify that 'AppName' is static for each text box, the test scripts below will work. Basically it instructs Selenium to find element whose name attribute contains "tAppName" (Watir can use Regular expression directly in finder, which I think it is better).

```
driver.find_element(:xpath, "//input[contains(@name, 'tAppName')]").send_key\
s("I still can")
```

Sending special keys such as Enter to an element or browser

You can use .send_keys method to send special keys (and combination) to a web control.

```
elem = driver.find_element("id", "user")
elem.clear
elem.send_keys("agileway")
sleep 1 # sleep for seeing the effect

# select all (Ctrl+A) then press backspace
elem.send_keys([:control, 'a'], :backspace)
sleep 1
elem.send_keys("testwisely")
sleep 1
elem.send_keys(:enter) # submit the form
```

Some common special keys:

```
:backspace
:delete
:tab
:control
:shift
:alt
:page_up
:arrow_down
:home
:end
:escape
:enter
:meta
:command
```

The full list can be found at Selenium::WebDriver::Keys documentation[1].

Use of unicode in test scripts

Selenium does support Unicode. Test script files containing unicode characters have to use UTF-8 encoding. This is easy to do, just insert `# encoding utf-8` at the beginning of test script files (*this is no longer required for Ruby 2.0 or later*).

---

[1]http://selenium.googlecode.com/svn/trunk/docs/api/rb/Selenium/WebDriver/Keys.html

```
# encoding: UTF-8

# ...

expect(driver.find_element(:id, "unicode_test").text).to eq("□□")
driver.find_element("id", "user").send_keys("проворный")
```

Extract a group of dynamic data : verify search results in order

The below is a sortable table, i.e., users can sort table columns in ascending or descending order by clicking the header.

Product ▲	Released	URL
BuildWise	2010	https://testwisely.com/buildwise
ClinicWise	2013	https://clinicwise.net
SiteWise CMS	2014	http://sitewisecms.com
TestWise	2007	https://testwisely.com/testwise

To verify sorting, we need to extract all the data in the sorted column then verify the data in desired order. Knowledge of coding with List or Array is required.

```
driver.find_element(:id, "heading_product").click  # first asc
first_cells = driver.find_elements(:xpath, "//tbody/tr/td[1]")
product_names = first_cells.collect{|x| x.text}
expect(product_names).to eq(product_names.sort)

driver.find_element(:id, "heading_product").click  # change sorting
sleep 0.5
first_cells = driver.find_elements(:xpath, "//tbody/tr/td[1]")
product_names = first_cells.collect{|x| x.text}
expect(product_names).to eq(product_names.sort.reverse)
```

This approach is not limited to data in tables. The below script extracts the scores from the elements like <span class='score'>98</span>.

```
score_elems = driver.find_elements(:xpath, "//div[@id='results']//span[@clas\
s='score']")
scores = score_elems.collect{|x| x.text.to_i }
# ...
```

Verify uniqueness of a set of data

Like the recipe above, extract data and store them in an array first, then compare the number of elements in the array with another one without duplicates.

```
second_cells = driver.find_elements(:xpath, "//tbody/tr/td[2]")
years_released = second_cells.collect{|x| x.text}
expect(years_released.size).to eq(years_released.uniq.size)
```

Extract dynamic visible data rows from a results table

Many web search forms have filtering options that hide unwanted result entries.

Product	Released	URL	
ClinicWise	2013	https://clinicwise.net	Like
BuildWise	2010	https://testwisely.com/buildwise	Like
SiteWise CMS	2014	http://sitewisecms.com	Like
TestWise	2007	https://testwisely.com/testwise	Like
		Displaying 1 - 4 of 4	

The test scripts below verify the first product name and click the corresponding 'Like' button.

```
driver.navigate.to(site_url.gsub("index.html", "data_grid.html"))
rows = driver.find_elements(:xpath, "//table[@id='grid']/tbody/tr")
expect(rows.count).to eq(4)
first_product_name = driver.find_element(:xpath, "//table[@id='grid']//tbody\
/tr[1]/td[1]").text
expect(first_product_name).to eq("ClinicWise")
driver.find_element(:xpath, "//table[@id='grid']//tbody/tr[1]/td/button").cl\
ick
```

Now check "Test automation products only" checkbox, and only two products are shown.

☑ Test automation products only

Product	Released	URL	
BuildWise	2010	https://testwisely.com/buildwise	Like
TestWise	2007	https://testwisely.com/testwise	Like
		Displaying 1 - 4 of 4	

```
driver.find_element(:id, "test_products_only_flag").click # Filter results
sleep 0.2
# Error: Element is not currently visible
driver.find_element(:xpath, "//table[@id='grid']//tbody/tr[1]/td/button").cl\
ick
```

The last test statement would fail with an error *Element is not currently visible*. After checking the "Test automation products only" checkbox, we see only 2 rows on screen. However, there are still 4 rows in the page, the other two are hidden.

```
▼ <tbody>
  ▶ <tr class="service_products" style="display: none;"></tr>
  ▶ <tr></tr>
  ▶ <tr class="service_products" style="display: none;"></tr>
  ▶ <tr></tr>
  </tbody>
```

The button identified by this XPath //table[@id='grid']//tbody/tr[1]/td/button is now a hidden one, therefore unable to click.

A solution is to extract the visible rows to an array, then we could check them by index.

```
displayed_rows = driver.find_elements(:xpath, "//table[@id='grid']//tbody/tr\
[not(contains(@style,'display: none'))]")
expect(displayed_rows.count).to eq(2)
first_row_elem = displayed_rows[0]   # first visible row
new_first_product_name = first_row_elem.find_element(:xpath, "td[1]").text
expect(new_first_product_name).to eq("BuildWise")
first_row_elem.find_element(:xpath, "td/button").click
```

Extract dynamic text following a pattern using Regex

To use dynamic data created from the application, e.g. receipt number, we need to extract them out. Ideally, those data are marked by dedicated IDs such as <span id='receipt_-number'></span>. However, it is not always the case, i.e., the data are mixed with other text.

The most commonly used approach (in programming) is to extract data with Regular Expression. Regular Expression (abbreviated *regex* or *regexp*) is a pattern of characters that finds matching text. Almost every programming language supports regular expression, with minor differences.

The test script below will extract "V7H67U" and "2015-11-9" from the text Your coupon code: V7H67U used by 2015-11-9, and enter the extracted coupon code in the text box.

```
driver.navigate.to(site_url + "/coupon.html")
driver.find_element(:id, "get_coupon_btn").click
coupon_text = driver.find_element(:id, "details").text
if coupon_text =~ /coupon code:\s+(\w+) used by\s([\d|-]+)/
  coupon_code = $1   # first captures group (\w+)
  expiry_date = $2
  driver.find_element(:name, "coupon").send_keys(coupon_code)
else
  raise "Error: no valid coupon returned"
end
```

Regular expression is very powerful and it does take some time to master it. To get it going for simple text matching, however, is not hard. Google 'ruby regular expression' shall return some good tutorials, and Rubular[2] is a helpful tool to let you try out regular expression online.

Quick extract pattern text in comments with Regex

The way shown in previous recipe is how typical regular expression is used in coding. Ruby's String[3] has built-in support for Regex to extract pattern text in a simpler way. For example, to extract the hidden version number (in comments) on a web page like below.

```
<!-- Version: 2.19.1.9798 -->
```

Just needs one line statement.

```
(driver.page_source)[/<!-- Version: (.*?) -->/, 1]
```

The (.?) is to match the text between <!-- and -->, and 1 is to return the first capturing group. If there is no match, nil is returned.

Here is a complete version of test script to verify the version number.

```
ver = (driver.page_source)[/<!-- Version: (.*?) -->/, 1]
puts ver # in format of 2.19.1.9798
expect(ver.split(".").length).to eq(4)
expect(ver.split(".")[0]).to eq("2")    # major version
expect(ver.split(".")[1]).to eq("19")   # minor version
```

How about extracting multiple occurrences of a pattern text in a web page?

```
<!-- TestWise Version: 4.7.1 -->
...
<!-- ClinicWise Version: 3.0.6 -->
```

Use String's scan method, which returns an array of matched text for a given pattern in Regex.

---

[2]http://rubular.com/
[3]http://ruby-doc.org/core-2.2.0/String.html#method-i-5B-5D

```ruby
app_vers = driver.page_source.scan(/<!-- (\w+) Version: (.*?) -->/)
puts app_vers.inspect  # [["TestWise", "4.7.1"], ["ClinicWise", "3.0.6"]]
expect(app_vers.size).to eq(2)
expect(app_vers.last).to eq(["ClinicWise", "3.0.6"])
```

21. Optimization

Working test scripts is just the first test step to successful test automation. As automated tests are executed often, and we all know the application changes frequently too. Therefore, it is important that we need our test scripts to be

- Fast
- Easy to read
- Concise

In this chapter, I will show some examples to optimize test scripts.

Assert text in page_source is faster than the text

To verify a piece of text on a web page, frequently for assertion, we can use `driver.page_-source` or `driver.find_element(:tag_name => "body").text`. Besides the obvious different output, there are big performance differences too. To get a text view (for a whole page or a web control), Webdriver needs to analyse the raw HTML to generate the text view, and it takes time. We usually do not notice that time when the raw HTML is small. However, for a large web page like the WebDriver standard[1] (over 430KB in file size), incorrect use of 'text view' will slow your test execution significantly.

```
driver.navigate.to(site_url + "/WebDriverStandard.html")
start_time = Time.now
expect(driver.find_element(:tag_name => "body").text).to include("language-n\
eutral wire protocol")
debug("Method 1: Search whole document text took #{Time.now - start_time} se\
conds")

start_time = Time.now
expect(driver.page_source).to include("language-neutral wire protocol")
debug("Method 2: Search whole document HTML took #{Time.now - start_time} se\
conds")
```

---

[1]http://www.w3.org/TR/webdriver/

Let's see the difference.

```
Method 1: Search page text took 8.44 seconds
Method 2: Search page HTML took 0.17 seconds
```

Getting text from more specific element is faster

A rule of thumb is that we save execution time by narrowing down a more specific control. The two assertion statements largely achieve the same purpose but with big difference in execution time.

```
expect(driver.find_element(:tag_name => "body").text).to include("language-n\
eutral wire protocol")
```

Execution time: **8.44** seconds

```
expect(driver.find_element(:id=> "abstract").text).to include("language-neut\
ral wire protocol")
```

Execution time: **0.05** seconds

Avoid programming if-else block code if possible

It is common that programmers write test scripts in a similar way as coding applications, while I cannot say it is wrong. For me, I prefer simple, concise and easy to read test scripts.

1. Reduce three line test statements to one by putting `if` or `unless` after the test statement

   ```
   if $verbose_mode
     puts "Page Title => #{driver.title}"
   end
   ```

   change to

```
puts driver.title if $verbose_mode
```

2. Replace if-else with ternary operator ? :

```
ticket_number = driver.find_element(:id, "ticket_no").text
if reference_number =~ /^VIP/    # special guest
  expect(driver.find_element(:id, "special_notes").text).to eq("Please go up\
stairs")
else
  expect(driver.find_element(:id, "special_notes").text).to eq("")
end
```

change to

```
expect(driver.find_element(:id, "special_notes").text).to eq(reference_numbe\
r =~ /^VIP/ ? "Please go upstairs" : "")
```

Use variable to cache not-changed data

Commonly, I saw people wrote tests like the below to check multiple texts on a page.

```
driver.navigate.to(site_url + "/WebDriverStandard.html")
expect(driver.find_element(:tag_name => "body").text).to include("Firefox")
expect(driver.find_element(:tag_name => "body").text).to include("chrome")
expect(driver.find_element(:tag_name => "body").text).to include("W3C")
```

Execution time: **25.9** seconds

The above three test statements are very inefficient, as every test statement calls driver.find_-element(:tag_name => "body").text, this can be a quite expensive operation when a web page is large.

Solution: use a variable to store the text (view) of the web page, a very common practice in programming.

```
the_page_text = driver.find_element(:tag_name => "body").text
expect(the_page_text).to include("Firefox")
expect(the_page_text).to include("chrome")
expect(the_page_text).to include("W3C")
```

Execution time: **8.3** seconds

As you can see, we get quite constant execution time no matter how many assertions we perform on that page, as long as the page text we are checking is not changing.

Enter large text into a text box

We commonly use send_keys to enter text into a text box. When the text string you want to enter is quite large, e.g. thousands of characters, try to avoid using send_keys, as it is not efficient. Here is an example.

```
long_str = "START" + '0' * 1024 * 5  + "END" # just over 5K
text_area_elem = driver.find_element(:id, "comments")
text_area_elem.send_keys(long_str)
```

Execution time: **3.8** seconds.

When this test is executed in Chrome, you can see a batch of text 'typed' into the text box. Furthermore, there might be a limited number of characters that WebDriver 'send' into a text box for browsers at one time. I have seen test scripts that broke long text into trunks and then sent them one by one, not elegant.

The **solution** is actually quite simple: using JavaScript.

```
driver.execute_script("document.getElementById('comments').value = arguments\
[0];", long_str)
```

Execution time: **0.02** seconds

Use Environment Variables to change test behaviours dynamically

Typically, there are more than one test environment we need to run automated tests against, and we might want to run the same test in different browsers now and then. I saw the test scripts like the below often in projects.

```
$SITE_URL = "https://physio.clinicwise.net"
# $SITE_URL = "http://demo.poolwise.net"
$TARGET_BROWSER = "chrome"
# $TARGET_BROWSER = "firefox"
driver = Selenium::WebDriver.for($TARGET_BROWSER.to_sym)
driver.navigate.to($SITE_URL)
```

It works like this: testers comment and uncomment a set of test statements to let test script run against different servers in different browsers. This is not an ideal approach, because it is inefficient, error prone and introducing unnecessary check-ins (changing test script files with no changes to testing logic).

A simple solution is to use agreed environment variables, so that the target server URL and browser type can be set externally, outside the test scripts.

```
# if not defined, will use default values after 'rescue'
$SITE_URL = ENV["ITE_URL"].to_s rescue "https://physio.clinicwise.net"
$TARGET_BROWSER = ENV["TARGET_BROWSER"].to_sym rescue :firefox
# ...
driver = Selenium::WebDriver.for($TARGET_BROWSER)
driver.navigate.to($SITE_URL)
```

For example, to run this test against another server in Chrome, run below commands.

```
> set TARGET_BROWSER=chrome
> set SITE_URL=http://yake.clinicwise.net
> rspec login_spec.rb
```

This approach is commonly used in Continuous Testing process.

Test web site in two languages

The test scripts below to test user authentication for two test sites, the same application in two languages: *http://physio.clinicwise.net* in English and *http://yake.clinicwise.net* in Chinese. While the business features are the same, the text shown on two sites are different, so are the test user accounts.

```
$SITE_URL = ENV["SITE_URL"] rescue "http://physio.clinicwise.net"
driver.navigate.to($SITE_URL)

if $SITE_URL =~ /physio/
  driver.find_element(:id, "username").send_keys("natalie")
  driver.find_element(:id, "password").send_keys("test")
  driver.find_element(:id, "signin_button").click
  expect(driver.page_source).to include("Signed in successfully.")
elsif $SITE_URL =~ /yake/
  driver.find_element(:id, "username").send_keys("tuo")
  driver.find_element(:id, "password").send_keys("test")
  driver.find_element(:id, "signin_button").click
  expect(driver.page_source).to include("□□□□")
end
```

Though the above test scripts work, it seems lengthy and repetitive.

```
def is_cn?
  $SITE_URL =~ /yake/
end

it "Test user authentication in both English and Chinese"
  driver.find_element(:id, "username").send_keys(is_cn? ? "tuo" : "natalie")
  driver.find_element(:id, "password").send_keys("test")
  driver.find_element(:id, "signin_button").click
  expect(driver.page_source).to include(is_cn? ? "□□□□": "Signed in successf\
ully.")
end
```

Using IDs can greatly save multi-language testing

When doing multi-language testing, try not to use the actual text on the page for
non user-entering operations. For example, the test statements are not optimal.

```
driver.find_element(:link, "Register").click
# or below with some programming logic ...
driver.find_element(:link, "Registre").click # french
driver.find_element(:link, "注册").click       # chinese
```

Using IDs is much simpler.

```
driver.find_element(:id, "register_link").click
```

This works for all languages.

Multi-language testing with lookups

```
# return the current language used on the site
def site_lang
  # ...
end

# in test case
if site_lang == "chinese"
  driver.find_element(:id, "username").send_keys("wang")
elsif site_lang == "french"
  driver.find_element(:id, "username").send_keys("dupont")
else # default to english
  driver.find_element(:id, "username").send_keys("natalie")
end

driver.find_element(:id, "password").send_keys("test")
driver.find_element(:id, "signin_button").click
```

If this is going to be used only once, the above is fine. However, these login test steps will be
used heavily, which will lead to lengthy and hard to maintain test scripts.

Solution: centralize the logic with lookups.

```ruby
def user_lookup(username)
  case site_lang
  when "chinese"
    "wang"
  when "french"
    "dupont"
  else
    "natalie"
  end
end


# in test case
driver.find_element(:id, "username").send_keys(user_lookup("natalie"))
driver.find_element(:id, "password").send_keys("test")
driver.find_element(:id, "signin_button").click
```

Astute readers may point out, "You over-simplify the cases, there surely will be more test users." Yes, that's true. I was trying to the simplest way to convey the lookup.

```ruby
user_lookups = {
  "natalie" => {"english"=>"natalie", "chinese"=>"wang", "french"=>"dupont"},
  "mark" => {"english"=>"mark", "chinese"=>"li", "french"=>"marc"},
  # ...
}
```

In summary, the test user in a chosen language (English in above example) is used as the key to look up for other languages. The equivalent user of "natalie" in French is "dupont".

Some, typically programmers, write the test scripts like the below.

```ruby
def get_admin_user
  # logic goes here
end


driver.find_element(:id, "username").send_keys(get_admin_user())
```

If there are only a handful users, it may be OK. But I often see hard-to-read test statements such as get_register_user_1() and get_manager_2(). Who is manager_2? Some test scripts go further to read test users from external configuration files, which are hard to maintain.

22. Gotchas

For the most part, Selenium WebDriver API is quite straightforward. My one sentence summary: find a element and perform an operation on it. Writing test scripts in Selenium WebDriver is much more than knowing the API, it involves programming, HTML, JavaScript and web browsers. There are cases that can be confusing to newcomers.

Test starts browser but no execution with blank screen

A very possible cause is that the version of installed Selenium WebDriver is not compatible with the version of your browser. Here is a screenshot of Firefox 41.0.2 started by a Selenium WebDriver 2.44.0 test.

The test hung there. After I upgraded Selenium WebDriver to 2.45, the test ran fine.

This can happen to Chrome too. With both browsers and Selenium WebDriver get updated quite frequently, in a matter of months, it is not that surprising to get the incompatibility issues. For test engineers who are not aware of this, it can be quite confusing as the tests might be running fine the day before and no changes have been made since.

Once knowing the cause, the solutions are easy:

- Upgrade both Selenium WebDriver and browsers to the latest version

Browsers such as Chrome usually turn on auto-upgrade by default, I suggest upgrading to the latest Selenium WebDriver several days after it is released.

- Lock Selenium Webdriver and browsers.

Turn off auto-upgrade in browser and be thoughtful on upgrading Selenium Webdriver.

Be aware of browser and driver changes

One day I found over 40 test failures (out of about 400) by surprise on the latest continuous testing build. There were little changes since the last build, in which all tests passed. I quickly figured out the cause: Chrome auto-upgraded to v44. Chrome 44 with the ChromeDriver 2.17 changed the behaviour of clicking hyperlinks. After clicking a link, sometimes test executions immediately continue to the next operation without waiting for the "clicking link" operation to finish.

```
driver.find_element(:id, "new_client").click
sleep 0.5 # hack for chrome v44, make sure the link is clicked
```

A week later, I noticed the only line in the change log of ChromeDriver v2.18:

```
"Changes include many bug fixes that allow ChromeDriver to work more reliabl\
y with Chrome 44+."
```

Failed to assert copied text in browser

To answer this, let's start with an example. What we see in a browser (Internet Explorer)

BOLD *Italic*

```
Text assertion
(new line before)!
```

is the result of rendering the page source (HTML) below in Internet Explorer:

```
<p id="text"> <b>BOLD</b> <i>Italic<i> </p>
<pre id="formatted">Text assertion  
(new line before)!</pre>
```

As you can see, there are differences. Test scripts can be written to check the text view (what we saw) on browsers or its raw page source (HTML). To complicate things a little more, old versions of browsers may return slightly different results.

Do not worry. As long as you understand that the text shown in browsers are coming from raw HTML source, and after a few attempts, this is usually not a problem. Here are the test scripts for checking text and source for above example:

```
# tags in source not in text
expect(driver.find_element(:tag_name, "body").text).to include("BOLD Italic")
expect(driver.page_source).to include("<b>BOLD</b> <i>Italic</i>")

# HTML entities in source but shown as space in text
expect(driver.find_element(:tag_name, "body").text).to include("assertion \\
n(new line before)")
expect(driver.find_element(:id, "formatted")["innerHTML"]).to include("asser\
tion  \n(new line before)");

# Note 2nd character after text 'assertion' is not a space character
expect(driver.page_source).to include("assertion \n(new line before)");
```

The same test works for Chrome, but not for IE

Chrome, Firefox and IE are different products and web browsers are very complex software. Comparing to other testing frameworks, Selenium WebDriver provides better support for all major browsers. Still there will be some operations work differently on one than another.

```
if driver.capabilities.browser_name == "firefox"
  # firefox specific test statement
elsif driver.capabilities.browser_name == "chrome"
  # chrome specific test statement
else
  raise "unsupported browser: #{driver.capabilities.browser_name}"
end
```

Some might say that it will require a lot of work. Yes, cross-browser testing is associated with more testing effort, obviously. However, from my observation, few IT managers acknowledge this. That's why cross-testing is talked a lot, but rarely gets done.

"unexpected tag name 'input'"

This is because there is another control matching your `find_element` and it is a different control type (`input` tag). For example,

```
<input type="checkbox" name="vip" value="on"> VIP?

<!-- ... -->
<select name="vip"/>
  <option value="true">Yes</option>
  <option value="false">No/option>
</select>
```

The intention of ths test script below's intention is to select 'Yes' in the dropdown list, but not aware of there is another checkbox control sharing exactly the same name attribute.

```
Selenium::WebDriver::Support::Select.new(driver.find_element(:name, "vip")).\
select_by(:text, "Yes")
```

Here is the error returned:

```
'ArgumentError: unexpected tag name "input"'
```

The solution is quite obvious after knowing the cause: change the locators, i.e. `find_element`.

A quite common scenario is as below: a hidden element and a checkbox element share the same ID and NAME attributes.

```
<input type="hidden" name="vip" value="false"/>
<!-- ... -->
<input type="checkbox" name="vip" value="on"> VIP?
```

In this case, there might be no error thrown. However, this can be more subtle, as the operation is applied to a different control.

Element is not clickable or not visible

Some controls such as textfields, even when they are not visible in the current browser window, Selenium WebDriver will move the focus to them. Some other controls such as buttons, may be not. In that case, though the element is found by `find_element`, it is not clickable.

The solution is to make the target control visible in browser.

1. Scroll the window to make the control visible

   Find out the control's position and scroll to it.

   ```
   elem = driver.find_element(:name, "submit_action_2")
   elem_pos = elem.location.y
   driver.execute_script("window.scroll(0, #{elem_pos})")
   ```

   Or scroll to the top / bottom of page.

   ```
   driver.execute_script("window.scrollTo(0, document.body.scrollHeight);")
   ```

2. A hack, call `send_keys` to a textfield nearby, if there is one.

Lack knowledge of the programming language

Unfamiliar to the programming language used for WebDriver tests can cause confusion too. For example, one tester came to me saying that his test scripts (shown below) was hanging for no apparent reasons.

```
sleep{1}
```

It turned out that it was a typo, resulting into a valid ruby code to execute a block (which sleeps indefinitely). He meant `sleep(1)`.

23. Extend Selenium

Selenium WebDriver provides a good solid API for automating web applications. When projects start to introduce Selenium, they often need to extend Selenium to better suit their environment (some companies refer people doing this as Test Automation Architects). In this chapter, I will show some test script examples in different syntax, while still using Selenium WebDriver underneath.

Watir-WebDriver

Watir-WebDriver[1] is a Watir implementation built on Selenium WebDriver, in other words, Watir syntax on top of Selenium. Watir is another free and open-source web test automation library, for testing IE. Many people like the simple and elegant syntax of Watir, but want to use Selenium's strength on multi-browser support. Watir-WebDriver fills the need. Watir-WebDriver is written by Jari Bakken who brought us the ruby binding for Selenium-WebDriver.

```ruby
require 'watir-webdriver'

describe "Same test on 3 different browsers" do

  it "Watir-WebDriver IE" do
    driver = Watir::Browser.new(:ie)
    driver.goto("http://testwisely.com/demo")
    driver.link(:text, "NetBank").click
    driver.text_field(:amount, "299" )
    driver.quit
  end


  it "Watir-WebDriver Firefox" do
    driver = Watir::Browser.new(:firefox)
```

---

[1] http://watirwebdriver.com/

```
      driver.goto("http://testwisely.com/demo")
      driver.link(:text, "NetBank").click
      driver.text_field(:amount, "299" )
      driver.quit
    end


  it "Watir-WebDriver Chrome" do
      driver = Watir::Browser.new(:chrome)
      driver.goto("http://testwisely.com/demo")
      driver.link(:text, "NetBank").click
      driver.text_field(:amount, "299" )
      driver.quit
    end
end
```

You can find more Watir examples in my other book 'Watir Recipes[2]'.

RWebSpec

RWebSpec[3] is a wrapper around Selenium and Watir. It provides an alternative syntax plus some useful utilities (like Selenium, RWebSpec is also free and open-source. Disclosure: I created RWebSpec). Here is a sample RWebSpec script.

```
require "rwebspec"
include RWebSpec::RSpecHelper
open_browser "http://www.google.com"
enter_text("q", "watir IDE")
click_button("Google Search")
```

One obvious difference from Watir or Selenium is that **RWebSpec test statements are in active voice**. Some might find the RWebSpec syntax is more concise and easier to read.

You may mix Watir or Selenium test statements in RWebSpec test scripts like below:

---

[2]https://leanpub.com/watir-recipes
[3]https://github.com/zhimin/rwebspec

```
driver.find_element(:name, "q").send_keys("Selenium full featured IDE")
click_button("Google Search").click # RWebSpec
```

Cross browser testing with RWebSpec: Watir for IE; Selenium for Chrome and Firefox

Cross browser testing has been talked a lot in recent years, but rarely done. Modern web sites are more complex and dynamic, there is NO perfect solution to automated test your web site in all browsers, simply because the browsers are different. There will be effort required for cross-browser testing, the more browser types you want to cover, the more effort you need to make.

Once we set out the context, Selenium is the clear leader on multi-browser support. However, Selenium IE Driver, in my opinion, is not satisfactory yet. Quite often, a test runs fine in Chrome, but failed in IE due to the web page not fully loaded (then I need add waits...).

Here is my approach to do crossing testing on three leading browsers: Chrome, IE and Firefox using RWebSpec:

- Use Watir for IE
- Use Selenium for Chrome and Firefox

RWebSpec provides high-level syntax (as well as the ability to call the driver underneath directly), which uses Watir or Selenium depending on the chosen browser type. Here is an example:

```
require 'watir'
require 'selenium-webdriver'
require 'rwebspec'

describe "Extend Selenium RWebSpec" do
  include RWebSpec::RSpecHelper

  before(:all) do
    # browser_type is a function returns browser_type, :ie, :firefox, :chrome
    open_browser :base_url => "http://testwisely.com/demo", :browser => brow\
ser_type
  end
```

```
after(:all) do
  driver.close unless debugging?
end

it "RWebSpec with AJAX" do
  click_link("NetBank")
  if RWebSpec.framework == "Watir"
  else
    browser.driver.manage().window().resize_to(1024, 768)
  end
  page_title.should == "NetBank"
  select_option("account", "Cheque")
  enter_text("amount", "123.54")
  click_button("Transfer")
  try_for(10) { page_text.should include("Receipt No") }
end

end
```

If you execute this sample test (*ch20_extend_rwebspec.rb*) in TestWise Pro edition, you can run the same test (without any changes) in three different browsers simply by selecting the browser type on the TestWise toolbar.

The test script is pretty much self explanatory. I have highlighted two items here:

1. **Changing the browser type**

   You may set the browser type in test scripts, such as

   ```
   open_browser :base_url => "http://testwisely.com/demo", :browser => :ie
   ```

   But this lacks flexibility. For example, you might want to run all tests against IE, Firefox and Chrome on the build machine 1, 2 and 3 respectively. browser_type function provides that flexibility by looking up an environment variable.

```ruby
# check environment variables to set browser type at run time
def browser_type
  if ENV['BROWSER_TYPE']
    ENV['BROWSER_TYPE'].to_sym
  else
    :chrome
  end
end
```

2. **Detecting the framework being used**

RWebSpec.framework returns the current web automation driver (Watir or Selenium) is being used. With it, we can use custom our test scripts for that specific driver. For example, the test script below set browser (Firefox or Chrome) size to 1024x768 with Selenium WebDriver, and leave the browser (IE) to its pre-set size with Watir.

```ruby
if RWebSpec.framework == "Watir"
  # ...
else
  browser.driver.manage().window().resize_to(1024, 768)
end
```

24. Selenium with Cucumber

Most of recipe tests are written in RSpec syntax, as explained in Chapter 1. There is another popular BDD framework: Cucumber[1]. You can find plenty of Cucumber tutorials on Internet. Here I will just provide a sample test project (in the sample recipe project available on the book's site) that you can run some cucumber tests right away.

This is how the receipt project looks like in TestWise.

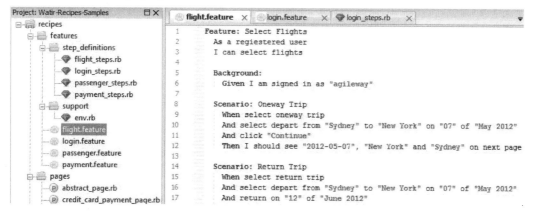

As you can see, there are more stuff than RSpec. There are four types of files:

- Features, e.g. *login.feature*. The top level test script file.
- Step definitions, e.g. *step_definitions/login_steps.rb*. This contains definitions (actual test steps driving the browser) for the steps in the features.
- Support files, e.g. *support/env.rb*. Usually just one *env.rb*, which sets up Cucumber's execution environment.
- Page classes, e.g. *pages/flight_page.rb* . This is optional, but a common practice to make writing and maintaining test easier. If you decide to write tests in RSpec and Cucumber, these page classes are reusable.

How Selenium-WebDriver is integrated with Cucumber?

The *support/env.rb* is the key file. The code fragment below in *env.rb* does four things:

---
[1]http://cukes.info/

- load selenium-webdriver gem
- load page classes
- initialize a selenium browser instance
- make the browser instance (@driver) available to step definitions via *Before* hook

```ruby
require 'selenium-webdriver'
require 'test/unit/assertions'

# Load page classess
require File.join(File.dirname(__FILE__), "..","..", "pages", "abstract_page\
.rb")
Dir["#{File.dirname(__FILE__)}/../../pages/*_page.rb"].each { |file| load fi\
le }

$BASE_URL = "http://travel.agileway.net"

# define a function to return the browser type to use
# (controlled by environment variable or other means)
def browser_type
  if ENV['BROWSER'] then
      ENV['BROWSER'].downcase.to_sym
  else
      RUBY_PLATFORM =~ /mingw/ ? "ie".to_sym : "firefox".to_sym
  end
end

driver = Selenium::WebDriver.for(browser_type)
World(Test::Unit::Assertions)

Before do
  @driver = driver
  @driver.goto($BASE_URL)
end
```

The `Before` hook is called before executing each scenario.

In step definitions (*_steps.rb*), we can directly use `@driver`.

```
Given /^I am on the home page$/ do
  @driver.navigate.to("http://travel.agileway.net")
end
```

I would suggest using page objects in step definitions, which will make test maintenance much easier.

```
When /^I enter "(.*?)" and "(.*?)" as passenger name$/ do |first_name, last_\
name|
  sleep 1
  @passenger_page = PassengerPage.new(@driver)
  @passenger_page.enter_first_name(first_name)
  @passenger_page.enter_last_name(last_name)
end
```

Execute Cucumber tests

From Command Line

As long as you have *cucumber* gem installed, you can run cucumber tests from command line.

```
cucumber features/login.feature
```

Here is a sample output:

```
Feature: User Authentication
  As a registered user
  I can log in

 Scenario: Registered user can log in successfully # features/login.feature:5
   Given I am on the home page  # features/step_definitions/login_steps.rb:9
   When enter user name "agileway" and password "testwise" # features/step_de\
finitions/login_steps.rb:13
   And click "Sign in" button    # features/step_definitions/login_steps.rb:18
   Then I am logged in           # features/step_definitions/login_steps.rb:22
```

```
1 scenario (1 passed)
4 steps (4 passed)
0m4.128s
```

Please be aware, cucumber execution can be a bit restrictive. You may assume the command below shall work:

```
cd features
cucumber login.feature
```

But it doesn't: reporting step definitions were not found.

```
1 scenario (1 undefined)
4 steps (4 undefined)
```

Work with Cucumber in IDE

Obviously this is tool-dependent. TestWise supports both RSpec and Cucumber, the way to execute tests are the same.

Besides executions, I found two useful features when working with Cucumber in IDE (taking TestWise as an example below):

- Generate step definition skeleton

  After writing the readable scenario, manually constructing step definitions is difficult (requires regular expression knowledge). In TestWise, just right click the feature file to generate:

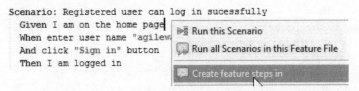

  Then enter the file name for the step file. TestWise will create this file with shown skeleton in the right location (under step_definitions)

- Navigate to step definition file from a scenario step

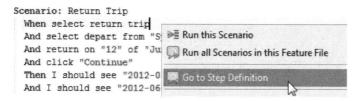

I think all tools claimed 'supporting Cucumber' should have these functions, check them out.

Cucumber or RSpec?

My short answer is: RSpec (with page classes) then Cucumber if Cucumber is a must.

Quite often, the choice of Cucumber is dictated by a manager who has little understanding of test automation. In this case, the benefits of Cucumber may not be realized but the team is hit with extra maintenance efforts. I have already covered this topic in my other book *Practical*

Web Test Automation[2].

[2]https://leanpub.com/practical-web-test-automation

25. Selenium Remote Control Server

Selenium Server, formerly known as Selenium Remote Control (RC) Server, allows testers to writes Selenium tests in their favourite language and execute them on another machine. The word 'remote' means that the test scripts and the target browser may not be on the same machine.

The Selenium Server is composed of two pieces: a server and a client.

- **Selenium Server**. A Java server which automatically launches, drives and kills browsers, with the target browser installed on the machine.
- **Client libraries**. Test scripts in tests' favourite language bindings, such as Ruby, Java and Python.

Selenium Server Installation

Make sure you have Java Runtime installed first. Download Selenium Server *selenium-server-standalone-{VERSION}.jar* from Selenium download page[1] and place it on the computer with the browser you want to test on. Then from the directory with the jar run the following from Command Line

```
java -jar selenium-server-standalone-2.40.0.jar
```

Sample output

---

[1]http://www.seleniumhq.org/download/

```
java -jar selenium-server-standalone-2.40.0.jar
Dec 29, 2014 2:47:08 PM org.openqa.grid.selenium.GridLauncher main
INFO: Launching a standalone server
14:47:14.387 INFO - Java: Apple Inc. 20.65-b04-462
14:47:14.387 INFO - OS: Mac OS X 10.9.1 x86_64
14:47:14.401 INFO - v2.40.0, with Core v2.40.0. Built from revision fbe29a9
```

There are two options you can pass to the server: timeout and browserTimeout.

```
java -jar selenium-server-standalone-2.40.0.jar -timeout=20 -browserTimeout=\
60
```

Execute tests in specified browser on another machine

Prerequisites:

- Make sure the Selenium Server is up and running.
- You can connect to the server via HTTP.
- Note down the server machine's IP address.

To change existing local Selenium tests (running on a local browser) to remote Selenium tests (running on a remote browser) is very easy, just update the initalization of Selenium::WebDriver as below:

```
driver = Selenium::WebDriver.for :remote, :url => "http://10.0.0.1:4444/wd/h\
ub", :desired_capabilities => :firefox
driver.navigate.to("http://testwisely.com/demo")
#...
driver.quit
```

The test scripts (client) is expected to terminate each browser session properly, calling `driver.quit`.

Of course, we can specify a different browser as long as it is installed and configured properly, on the remote server.

```
driver = Selenium::WebDriver.for :remote, :url => "http://10.0.0.1:4444/wd/h\
ub", :desired_capabilities => :chrome
```

Selenium Grid

Selenium Grid allows you to run Selenium tests in parallel to cut down the execution time.
Selenium Grid includes one hub and many nodes.

1. **Start the Hub**

   The hub receives the test requests and distributes them to the nodes.

   ```
   java -jar selenium-server-standalone-2.40.0.jar -role hub
   ```

2. **Start the nodes**

   A node gets tests from the hub and run them.

   ```
   java -jar selenium-server-standalone-2.40.0.jar -role node  -hub http://loca\
   lhost:4444/grid/register
   ```

   If you starts a node on another machine, replace *localhost* with the hub's IP address.

3. **Using grid to run tests**

   You need to change the test script to point to the driver to the hub.

   ```
   driver = Selenium::WebDriver.for(:remote,
     :url => "http://127.0.0.1:4444/wd/hub",
     :desired_capabilities => :chrome)
   # ...
   ```

   The usual way to run test from the command line:

   ```
   > rspec agile_travel_flight_spec.rb
   No examples found.

   Finished in 0.00014 seconds
   0 examples, 0 failures
   ```

   The test will run on one of the nodes. Please note that the timing and test case counts
   (from RSpec) returned is apparently not right.

Frankly, I haven't yet met anyone who is able to show me a working selenium-grid running
a fair number of UI selenium tests.

Here are my concerns with Selenium Grid:

- **Complexity**

  For every selenium grid node, you need to configure the node either by specifying
  command line parameters or a JSON file. Check out the Grid Wiki page[2] for details.

  It is my understanding that just pushing the tests to the hub, and it handles the rest
  based on the configuration. My experience tells me that it is too good to be true. For
  example, here is an error I got. While the error message is quite clear: no ChromeDriver
  installed. But on which node? Shouldn't the hub 'know' about that?

  ```
  [remote server] com.google.common.base.Preconditions(Preconditions.java):177\
  :in `checkState': The path to the driver executable must be set by the webdr\
  iver.chrome.driver system property; for more information, see http://code.go\
  ogle.com/p/selenium/wiki/ChromeDriver. The latest version can be downloaded \
  from http://chromedriver.storage.googleapis.com/index.html (java.lang.Illega\
  lStateException) (Selenium::WebDriver::Error::UnknownError)
  ```

- **Very limited control**

  Selenium-Grid comes with a web accessible console, in my view, very basic one. For
  instance, I created 2 nodes: one on Mac; the other on Windows 7 (the console displayed
  as 'VISTA').

---

[2]https://code.google.com/p/selenium/wiki/Grid2

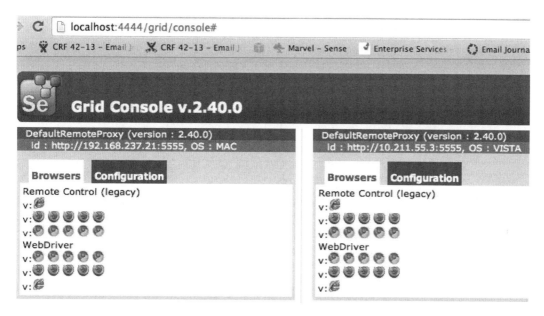

An IE icon for for Mac node? This does not seem right.

- **Lack of feedback**

  UI tests take time to execute, more tests means longer execution time. Selenium Grid's distribution model is to reduce that. Apart from the raw execution time, there is also the feedback time. The team would like to see the test results as soon as a test execution finishes on one node. Even better, when we pass the whole test suite to the hub, it will 'intelligently' run new or last failed tests first. Selenium Grid, in my view, falls short on this.

- **Lack of rerun**

  In a perfect world, all tests execute as expected every single time. But in reality, there are so many factors that could affect the test execution:
    - test statements didn't wait long enough for AJAX requests to complete (server on load)
    - browser crashes (it happens)
    - node runs out of disk space
    - virus scanning process started in background
    - windows self-installed an update
    - ...

  In this case, re-assign failed tests to anther node could save a potential good build.

My point is: I could quickly put together a demo with Selenium Grid running tests on different nodes (with different browsers), and the audience might be quite impressed. However, in reality, when you have a large number of UI test suites, the game is totally different. The whole process needs to be simple, stable, flexible and very importantly, being able to provide feedback quickly. In the true spirit of Agile, if there are tests failing, no code shall be allowed to check in. Now we are talking about the pressure …

How to achieve distributed test execution over multiple browsers? First of all, distributed test execution and cross browser testing are two different things. Distributed test execution speeds up test execution (could be just against single type of browser); while cross-browser testing is to verify the application's ability to work on a range of browsers. Yes, distributed test execution can be used to test against different browsers. But do get distributed test execution done solidly before worrying about the cross browser testing.

I firmly believe the UI test execution with feedback shall be a part of continuous integration (CI) process, just like running xUnit tests and the report shown on the CI server. It is OK for developers/testers to develop selenium tests in an IDE, in which they run one or a handful tests often. However, executing a large number of UI tests, which is time consuming, shall be done in the CI server.

The purpose of a prefect CI process: building the application to pass all tests, to be ready to production release. Distributed execution of UI tests with quick feedback, in my opinion, is an important feature of a CI Server. However, most CI servers in the market do not support this feature. You can find more information on this topic in my other book *Practical Web Test Automation*[3].

---

[3]https://leanpub.com/practical-web-test-automation

Afterword

First of all, if you haven't downloaded the recipe test scripts from the book site, I strongly recommend you to do so. It is free for readers who have purchased the ebook through Leanpub.

This book comes with two formats: *Ebook* and *Paper book*. I originally thought there won't be much demand for printed book, as the convenient 'search ability' of ebooks is good for this kind of solution books. However, during on-site consultation, I found some testers I worked with kept borrowing my printed proof-copy and wanted to buy it. It's why I released the paper book on Amazon as well.

Practice makes perfect

Like any other skills, you will get better at it by practising more.

- **Write tests**

  Many testers would like to practise test automation with Selenium WebDriver, but they don't have a good target application to write tests against. Here I make one of my applications available for you: ClinicWise sandbox site[4]. ClinicWise is a modern web application using popular web technologies such as AJAX and Bootstrap. I have written 437 Selenium WebDriver tests for ClinicWise. Execution of all tests takes more than 3 hours on a single machine. If you like, you can certainly practise writing tests against ClinicWise sandbox server.

  ClinicWise is also a show case of web applications designed for testing, which means it is easier to write automated tests against it. Our every Selenium test starts with calling a database reset: visit *http://sandbox.clinicwise.net/reset*, which will reset the database to a seeded state.

---

[4]http://sandbox.clinicwise.net

Wise Clinic sandbox

Database is reset. Current access token expires in 30 minutes   ×

| User name | Password | Sign in |

Forgot password?

User Logins (passwords: *test*)

Admin: admin
Therapists: mark*, jackie, tom
Receptions: natalie
Nurse: sharon

- **Improve programming skills**

  It requires programming skills to effectively use Selenium WebDriver. For readers with no programming background, the good news is that the programming knowledge required for writing test scripts is much less comparing to coding applications, as you have seen in this book. If you like learning with hands-on practices, check out Learn Ruby Programming by Examples[5].

Successful Test Automation

I believe that you are well equipped to cope with most testing scenarios if you have mastered the recipes in this book. However, this only applies to your ability to write individual tests. Successful test automation also requires developing and maintaining many automated test cases while software applications change frequently.

- **Maintain test scripts to keep up with application changes**

  Let's say you have 100 automated tests that all pass. The changes developers made in the next build will affect some of your tests. As this happens too often, many automated tests will fail. The only way to keep the test script maintainable is to adopt good test design practices (such as reusable functions and page objects) and efficient refactoring. Check out my other book *Practical Web Test Automation*[6].

---

[5]https://leanpub.com/learn-ruby-programming-by-examples-en
[6]https://leanpub.com/practical-web-test-automation

- **Shorten test execution time to get quick feedback**

  With growing number of test cases, so is the test execution time. This leads to a long feedback gap from the time programmers committed the code to the time test execution completes. If programmers continue to develop new features/fixes during the gap time, it can easily get into a tail-chasing problem. This will hurt the team's productivity badly. Executing automated tests in a Continuous Testing server with various techniques (such as distributing test to run in parallel) can greatly shorten the feedback time. *Practical Web Test Automation* has one chapter on this.

Best wishes for your test automation!

Resources

Books

- **Practical Web Test Automation**[7] by Zhimin Zhan

  Solving individual selenium challenges (what this book is for) is far from achieving test automation success. *Practical Web Test Automation* is the book to guide you to the test automation success, topics include:
  - Developing easy to read and maintain Watir/Selenium tests using next-generation functional testing tool
  - Page object model
  - Functional Testing Refactorings
  - Cross-browser testing against IE, Firefox and Chrome
  - Setting up continuous testing server to manage execution of a large number of automated UI tests
  - Requirement traceability matrix
  - Strategies on team collaboration and test automation adoption in projects and organizations
- **Watir Recipes**[8] by Zhimin Zhan

  While Selenium WebDriver is far more popular than Watir, in my opinion, Watir started real open-source testing for web applications. Learning Watir will help you design better test scripts. *(Jari Bakken, the author for selenium-webdriver gem, started with Watir, is also the author of watir-webdriver).*
- **Selenium WebDriver Recipes in Python**[9] by Zhimin Zhan

  Selenium WebDriver recipes in Python, a popular script language that is similar to Ruby.
- **Selenium WebDriver Recipes in Java**[10] by Zhimin Zhan

  Sometimes you might be required to write Selenium WebDriver tests in Java. Master Selenium WebDriver in Java quickly by leveraging this book.

---

[7]https://leanpub.com/practical-web-test-automation
[8]https://leanpub.com/watir-recipes
[9]https://leanpub.com/selenium-recipes-in-python
[10]https://leanpub.com/selenium-recipes-in-java

- **Selenium WebDriver Recipes in C#**[11] by Zhimin Zhan

  Selenium WebDriver recipe tests in C#, another popular language that is quite similar to Java.

- **Learn Ruby Programming by Examples**[12] by Zhimin Zhan and Courtney Zhan

  Master Ruby programming to empower you to write test scripts.

Web Sites

- **Selenium Ruby API**[13]

  The API has searchable interface, The *SearchContext* and *Element* class are particularly important:
    - SearchContext[14]
    - Element[15]
- **Selenium Home** (http://seleniumhq.org[16])
- **RSpec** (http://rspec.info[17])
- **Cucumber** (http://cukes.info[18])
- **Watir WebDriver** (http://watirwebdriver.com[19])

Tools

- **TestWise IDE** (http://testwisely.com/testwise[20])

  AgileWay's next generation functional testing IDE supports Selenium, Watir with RSpec and Cucumber. TestWise Community Edition is free.

- **Apatana Studio** (http://aptana.com[21])

  Free Eclipse based Web development IDE, supporting Ruby and RSpec.

---

[11]https://leanpub.com/selenium-recipes-in-csharp
[12]https://leanpub.com/learn-ruby-programming-by-examples-en
[13]http://selenium.googlecode.com/git/docs/api/rb/index.html
[14]http://selenium.googlecode.com/git/docs/api/rb/Selenium/WebDriver/SearchContext.html
[15]http://selenium.googlecode.com/git/docs/api/rb/Selenium/WebDriver/Element.html
[16]http://seleniumhq.org
[17]http://rspec.info
[18]http://cukes.info
[19]http://watirwebdriver.com
[20]http://testwisely.com/testwise
[21]http://aptana.com

- **BuildWise** (http://testwisely.com/buildwise[22])

  AgileWay's free and open-source continuous build server, purposely designed for running automated UI tests with quick feedback.

- **RubyShell** (http://testwisely.com/testwise/downloads[23])

  A pre-packaged installer for Ruby and automated testing gems including Selenium, RSpec and Cucumber. Free.

- **Ruby Installer for Windows** (http://rubyinstaller.org/[24])

  The standard Ruby Windows installer.

---

[22]http://testwisely.com/buildwise
[23]http://testwisely.com/testwise/downloads
[24]http://rubyinstaller.org/

15925908R00108

Printed in Great Britain
by Amazon